WHO'S LEADING WHOM?

The owner of a dog must become the leader of the pack, in the dog's mind. To do this, he or she must mimic the actions and attitudes of a leader and require the dog to recognize and conform to this. All areas of interaction must be choreographed by the owner, from when to pet, to where the dog sleeps, to who greets visitors or strangers first.

When a dog feels leadership coming from you, it will eventually:

- Be relieved to be free of the responsibility of controlling everything
- Feel more secure
- Develop more confidence
- Worry less about strangers
- Be more likely to interact happily with family and friends
- Be more obedient
- Show little or no aggression

LEADER
OF THE PACK

HOW TO TAKE CONTROL
OF YOUR RELATIONSHIP
WITH YOUR DOG

NANCY BAER and **STEVE DUNO**

HARPER

NEW YORK • LONDON • TORONTO • SYDNEY

HARPER

A paperback edition of this book was published in 2001 by HarperResource.

HarperCollins books may be purchased for educational, business, or sales promotional use. For information, please e-mail the Special Markets Department at SPsales@harpercollins.com.

Printed in the United States of America

Cover photographs copyright © 1996 by Don Mason

First Collins Lifestyle edition published 2005.

First printing: October 1996

Designed by Lili Schwartz

Library of Congress Cataloging-in-Publication Data

Baer, Nancy
     Leader of the pack: how to take control of your relationship with your dog / Nancy Baer and Steve Duno.
        p. cm.
  ISBN   0-06-101019-7 (pbk.)   ISBN   978-0-06-101019-4 (pbk.)
     1. Dogs—Training. 2. Dogs—Behavior. 3. Human-animal communication I. Dunno, Steve. II. Title
SF431.B325 1996
636.7—dc20   96-19490
                                                 CIP

HB 09.21.2023

This book is dedicated to
all those persons, past and present,
that we love dearly.

We would like to thank
our agent, Toni Lopopolo,
our editors, Maureen O'Neal and Lesly Atlas,
and our photographer, Don Mason.
Without them this book
would not have been possible.

Contents

Contents

INTRODUCTION

The familiar scent of white-tailed deer drifted over the six wolves as they rested in a small stand of scrub pines. The dominant female was the first to notice. She opened her eyes, raised her head, and sniffed the air, languidly at first, then with interest. As she rose, the dominant male, or "Alpha," opened his eyes and looked at her. He sampled the scent drifting through, then slowly rose. Quietly, the other wolves, two juveniles and two low-ranking females, made their way over to the dominant male. All stopped and turned into the wind, toward the deer. They came together, touched noses, and slowly headed toward the deer, the dominant male in the lead.

The wolves quietly approached a snow-covered clearing in the woods. Small plants broke the surface of the shallow snow in places. Two deer fed on the plants and on lichen growing on the trunk of a young scrub pine. One of the deer stopped, looked up, then continued feeding. At that moment the Alpha male sprung into the clearing, running full speed almost instantly. The dominant female leapt into the clearing from the opposite side, accompanied by the other four wolves. Both deer saw the Alpha male first and turned to flee, realizing their mistake too late. The dominant female closed the distance and leapt onto the back of the smaller deer. Quickly joined by one of the juvenile males and the Alpha male, the deer was quickly brought down and killed. The other wolves gave chase to the surviving deer but quickly withdrew, too excited by the fresh kill.

The Alpha male ate the deer's tongue, while the dominant female tore into the animal's hindquarters. They allowed the juveniles to join in, but when the two low-ranking females came too close, the Alpha male snarled them back. He would allow them to feed only after he, his mate, and the juveniles had fed sufficiently. The low-ranking females backed away, yipping in protest and hunger. After a few minutes, they again carefully approached. This time the leader allowed them to feed on the carcass. In an hour, the pack had consumed most of the deer. They lay *close to each other, cleaning themselves. Satiated, they would rest for a few minutes and then return to their favorite place, a half-mile into the forest, where they would sleep and play and celebrate their good luck. The Alpha male would lie quietly in his favorite place, a high spot near an old jack pine. He would watch the others and think of how much the young ones had learned in such a short time.*

This short scene illustrates more than a typical kill by a wolf pack. It demonstrates the efficiency of the pack and how leadership and cooperation are the key components necessary to the survival of the group. In the scene, the Alpha male, first alerted to the presence of prey by his mate, orchestrates and then leads a flawless, successful hunt, using experience, subtle communication, and an ingenious flanking tactic, evidence of the wolf's superior intelligence and planning skills. After the kill, he monitors the order of feeding. He and his mate eat first; they allow their growing offspring to join in. He requires the two subordinate females to wait, knowing there will be plenty left for them. He is not being cruel. He wants only to send forth the message that "this is what I deem proper; I want my mate and yearlings to begin first. When I am satisfied, then you will feed." Afterward, he leads the pack back to their resting place and lies down in his favorite spot, higher than the others. He is the leader of his pack; the others take comfort and feel secure.

A wolf pack is a socially stratified, highly disciplined group of related individuals who normally work together with remarkable efficiency. All members know their ranking in the pack and generally accept this without complaint. Wolves are highly social and develop strong emotional bonds within the pack. They are group hunters who tend to prey on animals larger than themselves. This reduces the number of kills necessary but requires a high level of intelligence and cooperation.

The most essential element for the survival of any group is the establishment of a system of law and order. This holds true as much for wolves as it does for humans. Order among wolves is established through a pack hierarchy. The pack order defines relationships within the group and provides the device that controls and directs the behavior of the members.

The pack order among wolves is a social "ladder" that ranks individuals, much like in the military. It is a tandem ladder, with males on one side and females on the other. An Alpha male and an Alpha female are perched atop each, with the Alpha male having ultimate say over all. These two Alphas are normally a monogamous, mated pair and are often the only producers of offspring in the pack, ensuring that only the strongest genes are passed on. Below them are subordinate males and females, peripheral pack members, and juveniles. Dominance in this hierarchy can and often does cross gender lines; the Alpha female is often dominant over subordinate males.

Capable leadership is essential to all aspects of wolf life, from hunting to mating to discipline. The leader of the pack is normally the largest, strongest, most demonstrative male, who achieves and maintains control over most pack interactions. The leader is always approached by other pack members with respect and diffidence. He initiates the hunt and determines the necessary tactics. He motivates the pack and stirs them into action. He is responsible for protecting the others and for fairly disciplining members who transgress the rules he has set. He is a benevolent dictator, whose goal is to maintain the most predictable and consistent environment possible. His confidence and leadership skills preserve the balance of things and limit conflict to a minimum.

To preserve his status, the Alpha male must continually assert his position. He must eat first, sleep highest, control his own space (and, to a degree, that of others), initiate interactions, and in general oversee the actions of the pack. He does these things instinctively; other members recognize his dominance, which further serves to affirm his position. Without regularly demonstrating his superior position, he might open up the possibility of a subordinate male challenging him for the leadership position. This would be disadvantageous to the pack, owing to the turmoil and anarchy that would accompany any struggle for power. A pack with stable, efficient leadership has the best chance at maintaining itself and raising its juveniles to maturity.

The allegiance to the pack hierarchy is instinctive in wolves. They know no other way to be. The same holds true for the domestic dog. Your dog, whether a Malamute or a Maltese, has the *same* pack instincts as its close cousin, the wolf. Humans have spent so much time with dogs over the centuries, however, that this instinct becomes easy to overlook. We tend to define our dogs in very human terms. This is understandable. Humans and dogs are both highly social creatures that cannot easily exist alone, without emotional ties. Dogs and humans share the same tribal, hunter/gatherer heritage; both are devoted to their young; and both have a complex system of communication. Humans and dogs are very much alike.

What is different is that whereas we have slowly evolved toward a more democratic social structure, dogs continue to remain instinctively loyal to an autocratic leader, holding a mind-set identical to that of their cousin, the wolf. Instead of belonging to a pack of wolves, however, your dog belongs to a pack of people. But there is no difference in how your dog relates to you or to another dog; in its mind, you are its own kind, and it must determine not only its ranking in the pack, but yours as well.

Owners who placate their dogs and make them the center of attention are telling their dogs that they are dominant. As far as a dog is concerned, only a leader would be treated this way. How do subordinates in the wolf pack treat the leader? They defer to him. They make him the center of attention. They treat him with respect, allow him to initiate interactions, and let him have his way.

When owners treat a dog democratically, allowing it to determine its own actions, they are unknowingly teaching the dog that it is the leader. And when a dog is the leader of the rest of its pack, does it not have the right and responsibility to discipline members of that pack when necessary? Of course it does. Think back to the Alpha wolf preventing the lower ranking members from feeding until he deemed it appropriate. He snarled them back for a few minutes. It was his responsibility to do that, not only to assert his power, but to ensure that the juveniles got enough food to maintain growth. He disciplined. Now, think of your dog. Do you feed it first, before you eat? Does it growl at you or other family members who try to touch its food bowl or chew toy? If this is the case, it is a textbook example of a dog that thinks it is dominant and therefore feels justified in disciplining a subordinate pack member (you or your child) for getting out of line. In its mind, it has done the right thing.

This type of situation is the cause of much aggressive behavior in dogs today. Many dogs have been taught by their owners to be the leaders of their packs. To determine whether your dog is one of those, ask yourself these questions:

- While on a walk, is your dog out in front, pulling you down the street?
- Does your dog go through doors ahead of you?
- Do you serve your dog dinner before you eat your own?
- Does your dog sleep with you?
- Do you wrestle or play tug-of-war with your dog and let it win?
- When visitors arrive, does your dog greet them before you do?
- Does your dog put up a fight if you try to cut its nails?
- Does your dog bump your hand to get petted? Do you then pet it?
- Do you let your dog choose the time and place for relieving itself?
- Must you repeat commands to get your dog to listen?
- Does your dog steal your possessions and then play keep-away?

If you have answered yes to a number of these questions, you may have unwittingly handed over the title of "leader of the pack" to your dog.

Over a million dog bites are reported in the United States each year. Many more go unreported. Most of the animals involved are not bad dogs. They are not crazy, rabid, genetically inferior, or possessed. Why, then, are biting and aggression in dogs such a common occurrence? The answer is that most of these dogs are doing only what they think they are supposed to do, what they have been unintentionally encouraged to do by the victims of those very bites.

The owners, by attempting to be accommodating, have actually taught their dogs to be the leaders of their packs.

Once allowed to assume the leadership role (often unknown to the owner until the onset of aggressive behavior), the dog will begin to set rules and boundaries and will discipline its "pack" as it sees fit. Discipline can take the form of barking, growling, snarling, or biting.

The dominant dog, in addition to disciplining, protects its position by coveting particular objects and areas and by initiating and terminating interactions with individuals in or out of the pack, when and where it sees fit. The controlling dog will tell the owner when it wants to be petted, when it wants to go out, where it wants to sleep, or when it wants to eat. It may never need to use overt aggression to keep its owner "in line." It can often get by with training its owner to give it what it wants, when it wants it, or by convincing the owner that, just like a human, "Bobo" just needs his space sometimes. This type of owner lives in a world of denial or outright ignorance and is reminded of his or her dog's dominance only when individuals from outside the "pack" (paper carriers, delivery persons, friends) attempt to interact with the dog, only to meet with an aggressive affront.

Owners such as these can eventually fall victim to aggression, usually when they have innocently invaded the dog's space or tried to retrieve an item of theirs from the dog, such as a shoe or sock. The dog is the "leader" and, in its mind, has the right to possess items and areas of its choice. When the naive owner tries to take back the item or tries to move the dog from under the coffee table or off the bed, the dog may bite. The owner will at first be confused and upset over the dog's behavior, the way a parent might be with a rebellious child. But in the dog's mind, it is the parent, and it is doing what is necessary for the good of the pack. The dog's subordinate (the owner) showed disrespect; discipline was called for and given, fairly, in the dog's mind.

The owner at this point may attempt to force the dog to obey. The dominant dog is thinking, "How dare you try to usurp my position!" A serious aggressive episode could follow, which is exactly what happens when a subordinate wolf attempts to move in on the

Alpha male's position. Confused and often scared, the owner usually backs off and calls in a professional behaviorist for help, puts the dog down, or takes it to the dog pound. All of this could have been avoided if the owner had learned how to communicate properly with his or her dog, using the dog's language, one that basically consists of posturing, positioning, and privilege.

The owner of a dog must become the leader of the pack, in the dog's mind. To do this, he or she must mimic the actions and attitudes of a leader and require the dog to recognize and conform to this. What works for an Alpha wolf will work for the owner. All areas of interaction must be choreographed by the owner, from when to pet, to where the dog sleeps, to who greets visitors or strangers first. When a dog feels leadership coming from you, it will eventually be all of the following:

1. Relieved to be free of the responsibility of controlling everything.
2. More secure.
3. More confident.
4. Less worried about strangers.
5. More likely to interact happily with family and friends.
6. More obedient.
7. Less aggressive (or not aggressive at all).

All dog owners want their pets to feel and act in these ways, don't they?

What This Book Offers

The Leader of the Pack is written by experienced behaviorists and is designed to teach you, the dog owner, simple techniques that will help establish you as the leader, thereby reducing disobedience and dominance aggression. These techniques are easy to perform and do not require you to have great training skills or participate in any type of physical confrontation with your dog. They are designed to create an atmosphere that mirrors the dynamics of a wolf pack, with the owner firmly in the lead. When they are performed correctly and adhered to, in 6 to 8 weeks you should begin to see a difference in your dog's behavior. Following an initial period of resistance, your dog will begin to understand the new rules and accept *you* as the leader. Once leadership is firmly established, the dog should happily obey, out of instinctive devotion to the pack hierarchy.

In addition to these exercises, we strongly recommend that you attend an obedience class with your dog. You will learn how to control your dog, how to use equipment, what a correction is, and when to give one. Also, a class will give you and your dog the opportunity to work together as a team, possibly for the first time. Remember, cooperation is essential to the pack's survival. Your dog instinctively knows this, and you should too. Obedience training can be a valuable tool used to attain leadership. The techniques we teach in this book can be accomplished with few if any corrections and without grabbing or physically manipulating the dog.

Some behavior books discuss using the "Alpha rollover," a technique involving physical intimidation through rolling the dog onto its back and assuming a superior posture over it. Although it can work effectively on young dogs if performed by a professional, it is a good way for the naive owner to traumatize a puppy or get severely bitten by an adult dog. We therefore do not recommend this practice. We also do not recommend other physical techniques for stopping a bad behavior, such as holding a dog's mouth shut if it is barking or biting. This is a great way to incite an aggressive dog into biting you.

This book can help you to get your dog to understand that you, the owner, are its leader. However, if you have a dog that is exhibiting severe aggressive tendencies, seek out professional help. Aggression can be genetically rooted. This type of situation necessitates the evaluation of a behaviorist who has years of experience.

One

LEADERS EAT FIRST

The old bull moose hadn't been an easy kill. Sick and lame, he still had been able to kick two of the younger male wolves into submission. One had a broken rib that would eventually heal but would hurt him through the winter. He would remember the old bull with each breath.

The Alpha male had led the attack. He had picked up the moose's scent an hour before and brought the entire pack down to the bank of a shallow stream. The old bull was standing in the middle, drinking. His rack of antlers still bore stray shards of their velvet covering, shed before the beginning of the mating season. The Alpha male and two younger males flew from the wooded bank and leapt onto the bull's back, tearing into him. The rest of the pack, including the Alpha female, attacked from the front and rear, biting and tearing at the legs and throat. The big bull had fought well but finally succumbed to a sustained, bone-crushing bite to the throat from the Alpha male.

The feeding began. Both Alphas fed first, allowing the two juveniles to join in. Two subordinate males and one lesser female waited close by, pacing and yipping in expectation. Slowly, they made their way over to the eight-hundred-pound carcass. There was more food than the entire pack could eat at a sitting, even if they gorged themselves. The Alpha male knew this and was anxious for all to feed, for it had been almost 5 days since the last kill. He knew there was more than enough food for everyone and that he would not have to worry about the order of feeding, this time. There was no need to worry about the juveniles getting enough.

He invited the lesser members to join in. They ate as much of the old bull as they could, leaving the rest for scavengers. The old bull had been

*the pack's hardest kill yet; the leader of the pack was proud of their
courage and hunting skills. He watched one of the juveniles feed on the
old bull's tough hindquarters.*

Feeding is an elemental drive, especially among carnivores. It
should come as no surprise, then, that the order in which pack
members eat is a fundamental indicator of the pack hierarchy. The
sooner a wolf eats, the more important it is in the pack. It is a great
honor to be able to eat first when all are hungry. In tribute to the
leader, the subordinate pack members must check their desire to eat
until the okay is given.

The Alpha wolf had been responsible for finding the moose,
choreographing the kill, and administering the final killing blow. His
competence and stature earned him the right to feed first and to
determine the feeding order for the rest of the pack. His mate and
their two most recent offspring were allowed to feed before the rest
of the pack. Their survival was of paramount importance to the
Alpha and to the species itself, for it was these wolves that would
make it possible to continue the leader's bloodline, which had been
consistently producing superior, competent wolves for generations.

There was more than enough food to go around, however, so the
Alpha quickly allowed the other pack members to join in. His plan
was never to selfishly hoard the food. That would have been
detrimental to the survival of the pack. Rather, he wanted to control
the order in which the wolves fed. The animals most important to
the survival of the pack (and of the species as a whole) ate first,
followed by animals of lesser importance and status.

The order of feeding is a primary indicator of status among
wolves. Apart from his concern for the survival of the key pack
members, the Alpha must also see to it that the leadership hierarchy
in the pack is judiciously maintained. He must eat first, not only to
ensure his survival, but also to send a signal to the others that states
"I am the leader; I am top dog, and to prove it, I am going to eat
before all of you." The order of feeding becomes a mirror image of
the pecking order in the pack. If the wolves fed chaotically with no
sense of decorum, the dominance hierarchy of the pack would
disintegrate and, with it, the ability for the members to work as a

team. It is precisely the ability of wolves to act as a cohesive unit that ensures their survival. Do anything to upset the pack dynamic and you threaten its very existence.

The leader of a pack *always eats first.* Period. That is his right. It indicates to those in and out of the pack just who the leader is. Humans, on the other hand, do not generally behave this way. The members of a human "pack" usually begin eating at the same time. Not surprisingly, most people also apply this practice to their dogs, feeding them when they themselves eat or, quite often, before. This is a big mistake.

Several years ago, two clients came to us for help in trying to solve a problem they were having with their two Miniature Poodles, Flora and Jazzy. Although they were wonderful people and caring owners, these clients unfortunately did not understand canine behavior at all and absolutely believed their dogs to be human beings, treating them as such. They eventually had to come to us for help, owing to acts of aggression that both dogs showed toward a small child.

John and Marie, both recently retired, loved Flora and Jazzy. They considered them the grandchildren they never had, and they would do anything to make them happy. When John came home from playing golf or visiting friends, Marie would set the table for dinner. She always set four places. Flora and Jazzy had their own high chairs and their own dinner plates on the table, piled high with their favorite canned food as well as some of whatever John and Marie were having. All four ate dinner together. Sometimes Flora would get up on the table and lick at the butter or walk over and eat out of Marie's plate. Flora and Jazzy always looked forward to dinnertime.

John and Marie had no conception that they were creating two little monsters out of their dogs. They had never experienced aggression from Flora and Jazzy, but they did not realize that it was simply because the dogs got whatever they wanted. The dogs were the leaders over their owners, and their leadership had never been contested; therefore, all was well. Not until someone from outside the pack became involved (in this case, a child) did problems surface. The child, a neighbor's niece, tried to stop Flora from eating her ice cream, which was on the table. Flora bit the little girl on the hand; the wound required six stitches to close. Although this was an extreme case (John and Marie did everything wrong and weren't quite in the real world), improper feeding practices *are* one of the many reasons that dogs begin to gain leadership over their owners.

First, we had to give John and Marie a primer on canine behavior. We tried to get them to understand that dogs and humans operate with a different set of priorities. Leadership and how it can be won or lost was explained, as was the importance of the owners' maintaining leadership in order to fend off conflict. Then we tackled the most glaring error in their dealings with Flora and Jazzy, namely, the feeding situation. Both dogs had attained dominance over their owners and therefore felt it was their innate right to eat anything they wanted. Anyone who was unlucky enough to get in the way of this supposed right risked being "disciplined" (bitten). John and Marie had never contested Flora and Jazzy's eating habits. They liked having them at the table, eating out of their dishes (to each his own). They therefore never incurred the wrath of these two little devils. When the child tried to stop Flora from eating her ice cream (a reasonable request), Flora bit her, thinking that the child was being insubordinate. Flora did what she thought she had to do, as leader. She wasn't intrinsically evil, just motivated to maintain her dominance by putting the child in her place.

After much cajoling, we convinced John and Marie to alter Flora and Jazzy's feeding habits. John and Marie had to eat their dinner first, while Flora and Jazzy watched from across the room, tethered to a doorknob to prevent them from coming over to the table. Afterward, the dogs' food was prepared and served to them in bowls placed on the kitchen floor, about 5 feet apart from each other. At no time were they ever again allowed to eat from the table. Flora and Jazzy's food was left down for 10 to 15 minutes, then removed. In this way, John and Marie began to take control of the feeding process, a major first step in gaining leadership.

Many of you, on coming home from a hard day's work, go right to your dog's dish, fill it with food, and bring your dog in from the yard to let it eat. To you, this is just common courtesy, a way of saying to your dog, "I missed you; here's your dinner." It is also convenient. After feeding your dog, you probably let it back out into the yard to eliminate and to get it out of the way so your own dinner can be prepared and served.

How does Bobo interpret this? He thinks, "You've come home to feed me. Good! Hurry, I'm hungry! Bring me my dinner, now, that's a good little sibling. Good job! Now, let me out, and feel free to fix something for yourself."

By feeding Bobo first, every morning or evening, you are unintentionally telling him that he is above you in the pack hierarchy. Remember, *leaders eat first.* Your dog knows this without being told. Even eating at the same time as you sends Bobo the wrong message, as does feeding him scraps from your dinner plate, at the dinner table. These practices equate your pack status with his and encourage him to rudely interrupt your dinner. Always remember, every interaction you have with your dog must indicate that you are above him in the pack hierarchy. The domestic dog does not need to hunt for food the way his wolf cousins do. You, the owner, provide it. The fact that it comes from you can be a powerful leadership tool if handled properly.

Goal: To Control the Feeding of Your Dog

1. You must determine the time and place for the feeding of your dog.
2. The feeding procedure must be orderly. The dog must *do something* in exchange for the food. A simple "sit" will suffice.
3. You must eat *before* your dog does. If possible, your dog should see *you eat first*, even if you have only a snack.

Solution: Feed Bobo After You Eat

From now on, eat *your* meal before Bobo eats. In fact, let him see you eat, from a position at least 6 to 10 feet away. If your dog does not know how to stay in a spot on command or becomes too excited or pushy and can't stay away from your table, put on his leash and tether him to a doorknob somewhere in sight of your dinner table. Then, ignore him while you enjoy your meal, even if he begins to bark or whine. If the barking gets out of hand, however, get a spray bottle (similar to ones used for misting house plants), fill it with water, set it on a tight stream, and spray Bobo right in the mouth, *from where you are sitting*. When you spray the dog, simultaneously say "no!" and then "quiet." Continue eating, and repeat the spraying if necessary, unless your dog enjoys the spray of water. This works for some dogs and not others. You may also try a loud, sudden sound. *Do not lose your temper or give in to the dog!* Adopt an attitude of stoic indifference.

Only after you are finished eating should it be Bobo's turn to eat. Prepare the dog's food, bring him over to the feeding area on a lead, have him sit, and then give him the food. Always have Bobo sit (or at least wait a few seconds, if the dog doesn't know how to sit yet) before putting the food bowl down. If Bobo tries to jump on you at this point, have a helper hold the lead and prevent the dog from jumping up on you. If you are alone, you will either have to hold the lead yourself in one hand, step on the lead, or use a squirt from the spray bottle as a consequence for the jumping. When spraying Bobo, say "no," and then "off." He should begin to get used to this new feeding procedure after a week or two, but he will not completely accept the new rules until after 6 to 8 weeks. If you remain consistent and committed, in about 6 weeks you will have taken a major step toward increasing your leadership status in the eyes of Bobo.

If you are having dominance or aggression problems, for the rest of your dog's life, you should feed your dog *after* you eat. If it is inconvenient for you to eat or you just don't have the time or appetite, then at least let the dog see you eat *something*, be it a cracker, cookie, or banana, before you feed it. And remember, always make Bobo do something (sit or wait) in exchange for the food.

Solution: Put Bobo on Regular Feedings

Free-feeding, or leaving food down all day for your dog, is not a great idea, for two reasons. First, when food is always available, it is not really *coming from you.* From Bobo's perspective, it is coming from the floor. In this way, you lose out on a tremendous tool for gaining a notch on the leadership scale. When you feed Bobo at specific times, the dog sees that the food is coming from you. The dog respects this. You become more important in your dog's eyes.

Second, dogs that free-feed tend to become picky eaters. Wolves do not free-feed; they eat when they make a kill, which may not be all that often. To them, eating is an exciting, heralded event. If food is always available, how exciting can it continue to be? A free-feeding dog will often pick throughout the day instead of eating everything at one or two short feedings. Its appetite becomes, at any given moment, lackluster at best. This type of dog also has less to look forward to during the day. Food motivation and the use of food as a training tool are both lost. In addition, free-feeders tend to become overweight, because they eat more overall, in many small, self-determined feedings instead of one or two defined feedings that you orchestrate. As a well-meaning owner who free-feeds, you may be replenishing the food in your dog's dish throughout the day and therefore have no clear idea of just how much your dog is eating.

Going from free-feeding to scheduled feeding should increase Bobo's desire for food. He will begin to look forward to the event of eating. You can effectively use his increased food drive in his training. A dog with a high food drive can be motivated to learn much faster than one with a lackluster appetite, simply because of its desire to get the treat reward.

Solution: Feed Multiple Dogs in Order of Dominance

The same rules apply here, with some minor additions. After owning two or three dogs for a while, you will probably have a good idea what *their* pack order is. Which dog is in charge? The one that always goes through doors first, gets to toys first, or greets people soonest is probably the dominant dog. Put the dominant dog's food down first. This will show that you, the leader, recognize that dog's dominance over the other dogs and that you understand the dynamics of their pack. Feeding the subordinate dog or dogs first would be disrespectful and might foment discontent.

If your dogs are aggressive to each other during feeding time or if one steals the other's food, it may be necessary to feed them separately, or to tether them apart from each other in the same room.

Solution: Feed Once or Twice Each Day

Feeding an adult dog twice per day is usually recommended, although many will only eat once per day and that is okay.

Try to keep Bobo at a constant weight that is healthy for him. There should not be a thick layer of fat over his body. You should be able to feel but not see his ribs, depending on the breed of your dog. Be careful not to underfeed your dog, as this could create stress and possibly food aggression. Bobo should feel full. Remember that, in the wild, wolves live a feast-or-famine lifestyle. When they eat, they do so until they are full.

Some dogs want to eat only once each day, and that is fine. If your dog is a large breed, however, such as a Great Dane, Mastiff, or Newfoundland, you *need* to separate the food into two feedings. These breeds normally eat at least 6 to 8 cups of food each day. We have found from experience that feeding more than 4 cups of food per meal greatly increases the chances of the dog's developing the condition known as *bloat*, or *stomach torsion*. It is a life-threatening condition whereby the stomach, filled with food and liquid, can produce digestive gases that twist the stomach, cutting off the flow of blood to major arteries. This condition is often fatal if not immediately tended to by a veterinarian. Large dogs should be fed no more than 4 cups per feeding, therefore. The food should be soaked beforehand with enough hot water to cover it. The food should soak up the water before it is served to the dog. The food will have expanded in the bowl instead of in the dog's gut, thereby reducing the buildup of digestive gases.

Some small dogs cannot get enough food in just one feeding to last them the whole day. If you have a small dog that is a finicky eater, consider feeding it twice each day; just ensure that it gets proper nutrition.

Solution: Handle the Dog's Food Bowl Fairly

Although you should have the right to pick up Bobo's food bowl without any threat of violence from your dog, we feel you have to be fair about it. Remember that in the wolf pack, once the entire pack is eating, the leader does not interfere with their meal. That would be unfair, and leaders are always fair. Problems with a dog being protective of its food bowl can be caused by an owner's handling the bowl too much during the dog's dinner. We had a client who did this with his male Kuvasz; each time the dog would begin eating, the owner would take the bowl away, make the dog sit, then give it back. How rude! The dog ended up becoming aggressive during feeding because of the utter frustration of the experience. You have to remember that dinnertime means a lot to a dog; it is probably the height of its day. Think of how annoying it is to have some big-headed dullard sitting in front of you in a movie theater on Friday night, talking and laughing out loud, ruining the only pleasure you have had all week.

From the time Bobo is a puppy, you should randomly drop a nice treat into his food bowl while he is eating, something like a piece of chicken or cheese. This will teach Bobo that the approach to his bowl by you or others is something to look forward to, rather than a time to worry about having its food taken away too soon. Eventually, while dropping the treat in, you can move the bowl around a bit, pick it up, and put it back down. Bobo will not see this as a threat if it is done properly.

Solution: Retrain a Food-Aggressive Dog

A dog that has a serious problem with anyone or anything that goes near its food bowl certainly does not respect its owner or see him or her as a leader. The owner of this type of dog needs to read this book and practice all the leadership exercises *religiously* in order to reduce the aggression and establish leadership. The help of an experienced animal behaviorist may also be needed.

In the meantime, there *is* something you can do to begin modifying this behavior. When you put the dog's food into a bowl and place the bowl on the floor, the food becomes a possession of the dog. At that point, when anyone or anything approaches, some dogs feel they have the right and the need to guard that food. To stop this guarding behavior, the following steps should be taken:

1. You must begin by feeding *all of your dog's food to it by hand,* for a period of about 2 weeks. Place your dog's food into a new bowl (many dogs become aggressive over their bowl), and put it on the kitchen table. Then, with you standing or sitting on a higher chair (like a bar stool), have Bobo sit in front of you. Feed him all of his food, handful by handful, until it is gone. If you don't feel safe feeding him by hand, you may at first drop it on the floor, one handful at a time, always waiting for him to look up to you for the next handful of food. He must depend on you to give him the food. You also want him to get enough food to feel full, even if you have to add vegetables to keep him from getting too fat. By using this technique, you never allow the dog to possess the food in its entirety. Rather, it is yours, and you are giving it to the dog. The food is now coming *directly* from you.

2. After 2 weeks of this feeding (yes, it is time-consuming but necessary), the procedure changes. Place the empty food bowl on the floor. Fill another bowl with Bobo's food, and hold that bowl in your hand or keep it on the counter. Take one handful of food out of *your* bowl and put it into the *dog's* bowl. Never give him more food until he eats what you gave him and looks to you for another handful. Continue feeding the dog one handful at a time until all the food is eaten and he is full. Use this technique for another 2 weeks or longer if needed.

3. The final step is to make Bobo sit and then put down his food bowl with food in it. While he is eating, place a piece of chicken or cheese in the bowl. Do this two or three times during the feeding, and continue to do this for the next 6 to 8 weeks. What you have done is to teach Bobo that the food is coming from you and that good things happen when you approach his bowl. If you stick to this plan and practice all the leadership exercises in this book, you should see the food aggression disappear. If it does not, see an animal behaviorist. Do not be confrontational or antagonistic with a food-aggressive dog. You will only make the situation worse, and you might get hurt.

Solution: Give Treats to Reinforce Behavior

Treats should be used to initiate and encourage new behaviors and to randomly reinforce existing ones. Don't use the dog's normal food. Instead, offer something special, such as a slice of hot dog or a strip of chicken. Treats can be great motivators, mainly because they are interpreted as positive reinforcement by Bobo, as opposed to a lead correction, which is negative. When first teaching a dog to sit, for example, we often bait the dog into a sitting position by slowly raising a treat up over and behind its head; most dogs will naturally raise up their heads, follow the treat up, and sit. At that point we praise the dog for a "good sit" and give the treat to the dog as a reward. Once the dog has learned the "sit," however, we reduce the number of treats given and supplement them with verbal or physical praise. The objective is to get the dog to work for *you*, not for a treat.

Whenever a treat is given to Bobo, *he must earn it.* Dogs that get gratis treats have actually trained their owners! A dog comes up to its owner, barks, then goes over and paws at the cabinet. What does the owner do? Opens the cabinet, pulls out the cookie box, and gives the dog a treat! Who's leading whom? Who's training whom?

From now on, whenever you intend to give Bobo a treat, toy, or anything desirable, *first make him do something to earn it!* A simple sit is plenty. By doing this, you show him that *you* are setting the rules, not he. That is what a leader does.

Be careful not to feed your dog too many treats during the day, not only from a training and leadership standpoint, but also from a health standpoint. Dogs that get too many treats end up getting fat and can eventually develop hip, back, or shoulder problems. Try using very small treats that Bobo can eat quickly. If you use too large a treat, he may forget all about what you want of him and lie down to finish the treat. Popcorn works well, as do slices of hot dogs. Remember, a treat is a privilege, not a right, and it must be earned by your dog. Bobo ultimately must work not for bribery but rather to please you.

Two

LEADERS INITIATE AND CONTROL INTERACTIONS

The Alpha male suns himself in the center of a small alpine meadow, savoring the warmth of the afternoon sun. A subordinate female leisurely grooms him, chewing and licking at parasites embedded in his hindquarters. He is grateful, and she feels at ease with him.

A 2-year-old subordinate male trots over, circles the resting pair, then casually flops down next to the female. The Alpha male lifts his head, looks straight at the young male, and lets out a low, almost inaudible growl, his lips pulled back ever so slightly from his teeth. He doesn't bother getting up. The female goes back to her grooming.

The young male's ears are flat back against his head, but he doesn't move. The Alpha continues his stare, now fully bearing his fangs. The young male averts his gaze, gets up slowly, and walks away, saving face and perhaps a bit more.

After a few minutes, the Alpha male gets up and shakes off, ending the grooming session. He gives the female a lick of appreciation and then runs over to where the rest of the pack is resting, playfully charging into the group and circling them quickly. The others get up and join him, romping and chasing him around the meadow, enjoying the last rays of the afternoon sun.

The leader of a wolf pack decides who can and cannot interact with him, when these interactions can begin, and when they should end. Because he is the leader, this is his right and responsibility. He must be fair and consistent about it, however, never overreacting or losing self-control. He also has the right to approach a lesser pack member and interact on his terms, whenever he deems it necessary.

With increased status comes increased privilege and responsibility. The leader must bear the responsibility to enjoy the privilege.

Domestic dogs obey the same rules as their wolf brethren. A dominant dog that fancies itself the leader will expect lesser members (including you) to groom it, pay attention to it, respond to its wishes, and leave it alone when it has had enough attention. A pushy, dominant dog will initiate and end play and decide when it wants to eat or eliminate or whose company is desirable or unwanted.

Owners of these dominant, pushy dogs often make the mistake of allowing their dogs to run the show, thinking that it is only right to let their dogs determine the substance of their day. This is a mistake. Dogs are not humans. If you allow your dog to determine when it will be petted, let out, or fed, or if you allow it to greet anyone it wants whenever it wants, then you are unintentionally giving up leadership to your dog. You are contributing to potentially delinquent behavior on its part.

The leader of a dog pack must determine what the protocol is in order to gain the respect of its subordinates. If any lesser member of the pack is allowed to set rules, leadership falls apart and nothing gets done. You are the leader of your pack, and you must therefore set the rules and determine the structure of your dog's day.

We have seen many examples of dogs controlling interactions with their owners. Last year, an owner brought his 2-year-old male German Shepherd to us because of its increasingly aggressive tendencies toward guests coming into the house. The owner sat on the sofa in our waiting room, his big dog sitting in front of him; the dog leaned his powerful body into the man, something dominant dogs (especially Rottweilers) like to do as a controlling technique. While the dog did this, the owner casually petted him, unknowingly rewarding him for the pushy, dominant behavior. When the man stopped petting the dog, the dog repeatedly bashed its head into the man's lap until the petting resumed. This is a textbook example of a dog initiating and controlling interactions with its owner. The dog was in effect *training the man to pet it*. The owner was a loyal subordinate and didn't even know it. His dog naturally assumed that he was the pack leader; therefore, when strangers came by, he felt *duty-bound* to confront them, to say "hey go away, you're not one of us." If the dog was allowed to continue this dominant behavior, the owner's authority would have been completely undermined. A biting incident could well have followed.

Goal: To Initiate and Supervise the Dog's Interactions

The owner must determine and supervise interactions the dog has with the outside world, including those with strangers, other animals, cars, and so on. If this goal is successfully completed, it will be a strong signal to the dog that you, the leader, are in charge. Relieving the dog of the responsibility of having to control things can often greatly reduce the animal's level of stress, help build confidence, and elevate the owner's status in the dog's eyes.

Before beginning the following exercises, make sure you have available an 8- to 10-foot lead to facilitate easy control in the home without having to resort to any type of physical confrontation. This lead will be referred to extensively throughout the book. It will allow you to control the dog's movements and location, a necessary requirement to establish leadership. The lead should be strong yet light; we recommend one made of cotton or nylon. In the beginning, your dog may chew on it. Nylon or cotton leads are inexpensive and can be replaced easily, unlike more expensive, leather leads. This lead will be on the dog quite a bit in the house, so make sure it is made of a material that will not mar your furniture if parts of it rub against it while your dog is walking through the home. It should have a clip at one end to attach easily to your dog's collar.

You will keep the lead on your dog for a 6- to 8-week period, except when you are not there to supervise. Leaving the lead on while you are gone could result in its catching on something and choking or injuring the dog. In addition to using the 8- to 10-foot lead, you should begin to locate areas in the home that this lead can be tethered to, such as doorknobs and table legs. We will be recommending some tethering of Bobo throughout the book, so find places that will be strong enough to hold up against his pulling.

Solution: Determine When to Take Your Dog Outside

You should determine when your dog gets to go out. If Bobo has taken control of when he comes and goes, you need to get that control back. Bobo should not be allowed to bark at you or scratch at the door or in any way tell you that he *has chosen* to go out. From now on you will determine the times for walking or for letting the dog out into the yard. If you are going to walk Bobo, make him sit first before the lead goes on, then reward him by walking him. If you are going to let him out into the yard, make him sit first before you open the door. The idea here is to make Bobo understand that he has to *earn* the privilege of going out by doing something for you, the leader. In this case, it is a simple sit (or anything else you decide on).

If Bobo attempts to initiate going outside by barking or scratching at the door, just ignore him. If he persists, tether him to a doorknob or spray him in the mouth with water from a plant sprayer. Remember, if Bobo is allowed to determine the time he goes out, he will want to go out whenever he fancies, which might be every 20 minutes, or when he hears a bird or a squirrel or the mail carrier. The end result is a loss of respect for you as a leader.

If you have a doggie door for Bobo, temporarily lock it in the closed position so that you alone will be in charge of when he goes out or comes in. If you have established regular feeding times for Bobo as recommended in Chapter 1, it should be easy to predict when he will need to go out to eliminate. Regular feeding promotes regular elimination with most dogs. We recommend that you set a schedule and keep to it. A typical schedule for going out would be the following:

- First thing in the morning
- Soon after each feeding (especially for puppies)
- Midday
- Right before bedtime

Three to four excursions should be enough, except for a puppy, who may need more frequent trips out. Remember, if you take your dog out too often, it won't become properly house-trained, which involves learning to hold off for extended periods of time. This often happens with dogs that have doggie doors.

Solution: Take Control of Physical Contact with Your Dog

Petting equals praise. Your dog should be petted, therefore, *only* after it has done something to earn it and not when *it* decides it wants to be petted. A controlling, or dominant, dog will come up to its owner, lean into him or her, and say, "Here I am; pet me until I've had enough." When this type of dominant dog is satisfied, it will wander off, just the way the Alpha wolf did in the opening scenario of this chapter. It allowed the subordinate female to groom (or pet) it, then ended the session when it so desired. Follow these simple rules:

1. If your dog attempts to cajole you into petting it, *ignore it and walk away.*
2. When you decide it is time to pet the dog, make it do one simple thing first, such as a sit. Then pet and praise it. Make the dog *earn* your attention.
3. *You* should decide when to end the petting session. When you do, just say "good, Bobo" and walk away. Remember always *to initiate and end the petting yourself,* to *ignore* the dog when it tries to initiate, and to praise *only when the dog has done something to earn it.*

As the leader of your pack, you have the right to handle your dog whenever you want. Many breeds require regular brushing to prevent matting of the coat, and all breeds need to have their nails cut on a regular basis. In addition, both you and your vet need to be able to examine your dog for any abnormalities. It is necessary, therefore, for your dog to accept handling as part of the normal routine.

Many dominant dogs will not allow you or anyone else to perform these procedures. In the wolf pack, the dominant animal does not let others touch it unless it desires to be touched. Only submissive dogs would permit others to handle them whenever they want to. If Bobo balks at the idea of being brushed, examined, petted while he sleeps, or having his nails cut, you probably have a leadership problem. Inherently dominant breeds such as the Rottweiler, Bullmastiff, Shar Pei, or Chow Chow are especially bad when it comes to tolerating handling, especially having their nails clipped.

GROOMING YOUR DOG

Ideally, grooming should start when Bobo is a puppy. It is never too late, however, so don't exclude your adolescent or adult dog from this exercise. The key to getting Bobo to accept being touched is to make it a positive experience. Yelling or getting physical with Bobo will only make him dread the experience.

1. Attach a leash to Bobo, and hold it in one hand with the dog standing in front of you. (An alternative is to tether the leash to a doorknob; this will free up your left hand.) You may want to be in a crouching position or on your knees. Also, have some small treats on hand. Puppies can be held in your lap or in front of you.

2. With one hand, lightly brush Bobo's coat with a brush while simultaneously offering him a treat with your other hand. Make sure you cover all areas of the dog that need brushing, including the tail, ears, and chin. Talk positively to him, but do not allow him to attempt running away. If he puts up a fight, just say *no* while giving the leash a slight pop. The objective is to get your dog to look forward to these brushing sessions. If Bobo is a matted mess, it might be a good idea to take him to a groomer and have him shaved down, thereby preventing the brushing procedure from becoming an almost impossible struggle. If you don't feel safe doing any grooming, seek professional help.

CLIPPING YOUR DOG'S NAILS

Nail clipping can be a difficult procedure for many adult dogs. Most animals do not like having their feet touched; feet are a primary means of escape and are therefore protected and guarded. Nails do need to be periodically trimmed, however. If left to grow unchecked, they can distort the placement of the dog's foot enough to eventually cause structural problems, including arthritis. Again, it is best to begin practicing this procedure when the dog is just a pup.

1. Begin by simply picking up Bobo's front feet, one at a time, and praising him, as if you were trying to teach him to shake. Each time, reward him with a treat. Gradually lengthen the time that you handle each foot, and allow your examination gradually to become more thorough. Handle each individual toe, and touch each nail. Do the same with the back feet as well. You may find it easier to do this with Bobo lying down. Work this stage of the exercise twice each day for several days before moving on.

2. During the handling of Bobo's feet, begin touching his nails with the nail clippers. The feel of metal on their nails can worry some dogs, so go slowly, and continue to reward with treats. Repeat this step for several days before moving on.

3. Once Bobo accepts being touched on the nails with the clippers, it is time to begin trimming. Do only one or two nails per session at first. You should cut off only the very tips of the nails (about an eighth of an inch) so that you can get the hang of it without risking "quicking" the nail, or cutting it too short, which results in bleeding and pain for the dog. If you "quick" Bobo at this stage, he might never trust you to do this again, so be conservative. Don't let the procedure take too long, however; learn to be precise and quick. Make it seem like an everyday thing to the dog. If you act nervous, Bobo will pick up on it and mirror your concern. After cutting the nails on each foot, reward the dog with a treat.

Warning: An extremely worried or dominant/aggressive dog may not allow you to cut its nails and may try to bite if you persist. If your dog is at this stage, do not attempt to cut its nails, and consider seeking out the help of a professional canine behaviorist.

CHECKING YOUR DOG'S EARS AND MOUTH

Breeds such as the Cocker Spaniel or Basset Hound need to have their ears cleaned on a regular basis to prevent infection and excessive odor. You may also have to check periodically on the condition of your dog's gums and teeth. It is important to be able to accomplish these tasks without the dog's putting up a fight. Go slowly, and be patient. If you are unable to do these things successfully, seek professional help.

1. Have Bobo sit in front of you. Praise him for a "good sit," and give him a treat. Pet him on the head, and slowly allow this petting to extend to his ears. Stroke his ears and praise him. After a minute or so, casually lift an ear and examine the inside. Then, repeat this sequence with the other ear. Continue until you can easily put a finger in each ear, gently rubbing the inside. Most dogs enjoy this.
2. Once you have mastered the first step, you will want to replace your finger with a cotton swab that has been dipped in a small amount of mineral oil. Mineral oil will loosen any oily, waxy deposits in the ear. After swabbing the ear with the oiled swab, repeat the procedure with a dry one. Then, clean the other ear. Throughout this procedure, make sure you praise Bobo and intermittently give him treats. Do not praise him if he growls or misbehaves in any way.

MASSAGING YOUR DOG

We had a client come in last year for help with his pet Chow Chow, named Shing-Shing. No one, including the owner, could pet Shing-Shing without eliciting at least a growl from him; often, he would even snap at people. This behavior can happen with Chow Chows; some do not like to be touched, particularly on the head, an area where most people attempt to pet a dog. After determining that the dog was not in any physical pain, we had the owner leave Shing-Shing with us for a 2-week stay. In addition to working the dog on basic obedience skills, we began desensitizing him to touch through the use of massage. At first we needed to muzzle him; he simply could not imagine that being touched could be a pleasurable experience. After a few days, however, he began to enjoy it. We had started with a light neck rub and gradually moved on to massage of the back, chest, legs, and feet. By the end of the 2-week period, he couldn't get enough of it, and he would let us pet him on the head whenever we wanted to. The owner came in for several lessons and was shocked at the change. He continued the daily massages and even got the rest of the family involved. Shing-Shing has stopped growling completely.

Massage is an excellent way to get a recalcitrant dog to accept handling. It has a calming, relaxing effect on most dogs and is interpreted by them as petting, something they like. An easy way to gain a dog's confidence, massage can help you establish a proper physical relationship with your dog. Many dominant dogs that balk at being handled or brushed gladly accept massage. Nervous, skittish dogs also respond well to massage; a feeling of mutual trust is fostered, often resulting in increased confidence and respect.

1. Start at the head of your dog. Go from stroking the head to lightly rubbing the neck, a location for stress in both dogs and humans. While massaging, speak quietly and positively to Bobo. Take your time, and don't move on to the rest of the body until Bobo has accepted massage around the head and neck. With some dogs you are better off starting on the dog's rump and work up to the head, such as the Chow Chow.
2. Next, begin to work your way down Bobo's back, using light circular motions. Go up and down, quietly talking to Bobo the whole time. Work the back and neck for several sessions before moving on.
3. While one hand is going down the back, begin lightly massaging the dog's chest or shoulders with your other hand. Eventually,

you want to cover the dog's entire body, including the legs and feet. Make it an enjoyable experience for your dog.

Solution: Train Your Dog to Greet Properly

A dominant dog will want to initiate contact with outsiders, including animals and persons outside of your family. If your dog thinks it is the leader, it will feel obligated to rush up to strangers and (depending on the breed, the dog's heredity, and its behavioral history) either greet them happily or openly challenge their right to be in its space. Either way, it can be an obnoxious experience. We have had clients with large, friendly dogs that, while out on walks, will spot a neighbor it likes and drag its hapless owner half a block to say hello. Although comical, this is nonetheless a sign of ineffective leadership, and it could lead to injury.

A worst-case scenario is the dominant dog that is highly territorial and suspicious of strangers. We once worked with the owners of a Chinese Shar Pei that was extremely dog-aggressive. The owners lived in a quiet, rural neighborhood and used to let the dog lie in the driveway during the day, with no fence or barrier of any sort. One day, the neighbor's Cocker Spaniel got out of its yard and wandered over to the Shar Pei's house. The Shar Pei attacked and literally ripped it to pieces.

The owners of this dog made a number of errors. First, they chose an extremely dominant, combative breed. Second, they allowed it *far* too much freedom and did not supervise it during the day. Third, the dog had never been socialized with persons or animals outside of the family. Consequently, the dog established himself as the leader, and when that poor little noisy Cocker came over and invaded the Shar Pei's territory, the result was inevitable.

One of the most important things you can do with your young dog is to socialize it with people and animals as much as possible. This socialization should be a positive experience so that the dog learns it has nothing to fear and everything to gain, including increased confidence and trust. The socialization, however, must occur according to *your rules*. You must decide when the greeting starts, when it ends, and how it proceeds.

GREETING PEOPLE

You should begin to teach Bobo to look forward to the approach of strangers through the use of treats. Throughout the exercise, you should remain calm and try not to tighten your grip on the lead; doing so signals your nervousness to Bobo and may cause him to become worried.

The following exercise can be done in the home or outside. If Bobo is very territorial, however, work him outside on neutral territory. It also is helpful if your dog knows how to sit on command. (Remember that in conjunction with reading this book, we heartily recommend that you also attend a basic obedience class.)

1. Have Bobo on a 6-foot leash. Also, have some treats in your pocket. A friend should be standing about 10 to 15 feet away from you and your dog.
2. Ask Bobo to sit, and give him a treat. Have your friend approach, with the intention of greeting *you*, not the dog. Remember, if you are the leader of your pack, then *you*, like the Alpha wolf, are responsible for initiating interactions with the outside world. As your friend approaches, attempt to keep Bobo in a sitting position. If he breaks the position, say *no* and instruct your friend to walk away. Place Bobo back into a sit, and try again. You want your dog eventually to remain in the sitting position while your friend approaches and greets *you*, saying hello and shaking your hand. You may have to repeat the exercise five or ten times before Bobo understands. When he finally does remain in the sitting position through the greeting, praise him and give him a treat.
3. Next, have your friend give Bobo a friendly pat on the head while he remains in the sit position. (If your dog shows *any* signs of aggression or fear at this point or is averse to being petted, *do not* have your friend physically pet it. Instead, have

your friend verbally praise Bobo for a good sit and perhaps drop a treat at his feet. It is okay if the dog breaks its sit to eat the treat.) Your friend should maintain an upright posture throughout the entire exercise. Repeat the exercise until your friend can pet and praise Bobo without his breaking the sit position.

The whole objective of this exercise is for you to orchestrate a controlled, nonthreatening greeting between your dog and your friend, on your terms. Work this at least once each day, and try to use different friends if you can so that the dog becomes used to different body types.

GREETING OTHER DOGS

When two dogs meet, they always go through a predictable posturing ritual to determine quickly who is dominant and who is subordinate. This is normal and should not be discouraged. Dogs that have been allowed to run the house, however, may have an inflated sense of importance and may learn to become abnormally territorial and aggressive toward other dogs, especially within the boundaries of their own territory.

Before we continue this section on greeting other dogs, we insert a brief discussion of aggression in its different forms so that you might better understand its causes and possible remedies. The causes of aggression are numerous. We have separated aggression into five different categories: genetic, fear-based, territorial, competitive, and possessive. Dogs that show aggression can fit into one or more of these categories.

Genetic Aggression

Some dogs inherit from their parents a potential toward aggression, although this type of aggression is not as common as the other types. Dogs that inherit aggressive tendencies from their ancestors are very hard, if not impossible, to change; the behavior can be modified to an extent, but the predisposition will always be there in the dog. The only way to determine whether a dog is genetically predisposed to aggression is to observe carefully its parents, grandparents, and siblings for any type of aberrant, antisocial behavior. If profound aggressive tendencies are observed in one or more of the dog's family members, the chances of inherited aggression are heightened substantially. If you see signs of aggression in any of them, find yourself another breeder.

Some breeds are more prone to aggression than others. Rottweilers, Chows, Akitas, Pit Bulls, Chinese Shar Peis, Australian Cattle Dogs, Bloodhounds, Bernese Mountain Dogs, Lhasa Apsos, Bouviers, and Miniature Pinschers are breeds that have recent reputations for being genetically predisposed toward aggression, primarily because of bad breeding practices. Irresponsible breeders often put physical appearance over temperament when choosing breeding stock, which leads to a degradation of the breed quality. This is not to say that all dogs of the breeds listed are aggressive; it largely depends on the integrity of the breeder.

Genetically aggressive dogs often attack another dog or a person without provocation. The inability to predict when one of these dogs will "fire up" is what makes them so dangerous. Pack loyalties often do not prevent a dog like this from attacking; no one is immune from this type of threat. These dogs are the "Ted Bundys" of the canine world; no amount of behavior modification can ensure that they won't do some person or animal irreparable harm.

Some dogs are born with a very high prey drive. This form of aggression is predominantly a hereditary trait, although it can be exaggerated through behavior modification. (We of course advise you *never to try to get Bobo to attack another animal.*) Sight hounds, for example, have an instinctive desire to chase down small animals such as rabbits. Many dogs in the hound category are driven to chase down fox, badgers, or other small game. Terriers, of course, have an insatiable desire to track down and kill rodents. This instinctive behavior was bred into many breeds of dogs so that they could aid people in hunting and in the elimination of vermin. Once a dog shows a profoundly high prey drive toward other animals, the drive is almost impossible to eliminate. The best you can do is to keep the dog on-lead and limit its exposure to animals that you know it will want to chase down and kill. If you have a Rottweiler or a Siberian Husky, for example, don't let it off-leash in a park that has a little Toy Poodle running around. It would also be a bad idea to adopt a small kitten and bring it into a house that has a dog with a high prey drive living there. Chances are the poor little thing wouldn't last the night.

Fear-Based Aggression

One of the most common causes of aggression, fear will motivate a dog to fight or attack if it thinks its life is in jeopardy. Many dogs that exhibit signs of fear aggression have had some traumatic event occur to them at a very early age. For instance, a puppy that was stepped on accidentally by a child when it was only 8 weeks old might carry an irrational fear of children into its adult life and show aggressive tendencies to any child who comes near it, no matter how benign its behavior toward the dog. Other dogs develop a fearful aggression toward other dogs if they are removed from their litter before the age of 7 weeks. The 6- to 7-week-old period is crucial to the development of social skills in all canines. If a puppy does not get to socialize with its littermates during this time, it may not be able to deal maturely with other dogs later in life. What a dog does not understand, it fears, and what it fears it must either avoid or fight.

Fear aggression can also be caused by putting a shy or timid dog into a stressful situation. If you know that your dog is afraid of tall men with hats, for example, then by all means don't force the dog to tolerate being petted by someone fitting this description. You are only setting your dog up to fail; this is not the sign of good leadership. Likewise, a shy or timid dog that has a weak, insecure, or fearful owner is much more likely to show fear-based aggression than the same dog with a confident, take-charge kind of owner. This is why we don't usually encourage overly timid, fearful, or frail individuals to purchase a dog. Many frightened people get dogs for protection, but they fail to realize that without confident leadership, their dogs may be insecure worriers that won't be capable of dealing with a true threat. This type of dog is much more likely to run away from trouble.

Although it is caused in part by genetic factors, fear aggression in dogs can be worked with to bring the aberrant behavior into check. A combination of strong, confident leadership and gradual desensitization to frightening stimuli can lessen the chances of an aggressive event. The owner of a fearful dog must admit to his or her dog's limitations, however, and know what situations to avoid. If Bobo is scared to death of walking down a busy city street, for example, then simply avoid that situation. Walk him down a quieter street with some activity instead. There is no shame in admitting that your dog just can't deal with certain events.

Territorial Aggression

A combination of heredity and learned behavior, territorial aggression can be more pronounced in certain breeds. Rottweilers, German Shepherds, Mastiffs, Pit Bulls, Akitas, Chihuahuas, Australian Cattle Dogs, and Chows are breeds that tend to be quite territorial by nature. Other breeds can be just as protective of their territories, however, depending on the dog's environment and upbringing. If a dog is kept on a chain in a yard all day and is continually teased by children in the yard next door, you can be sure that it will have an extremely territorial nature.

Territorial aggression in your dog can be kept to a minimum if you become a competent, capable leader. If you make it clear to Bobo that the home, car, and yard are your places and that you are perfectly able to defend them yourself, he will be less likely to show territorial aggression toward another person or dog. Pushy, dominant dogs tend to be overly territorial. By establishing yourself as the leader, you will diminish Bobo's pushiness and with it much of his territorial concern.

Competitive Aggression

When two dogs are very close to each other in the pecking order, quite often they have dominance contests that may erupt into overt aggression. These bouts usually look and sound worse than they really are. Most of the time they are over as quickly as they began, with no physical harm done. If two dogs of similar status come into a room and find a bone on the floor, for instance, they may fight over it briefly. Eventually, however, the two dogs will come to some understanding with regard to who is higher in the pecking order; once this happens, the aggression usually subsides.

An exception to this rule is female-to-female competition; although male dogs often put on quite a ferocious show, most of it is simply harmless posturing. It is the females that really mean business. Females seem to have a fiercer rivalry than their male counterparts; fights between them often end in a trip to the vet for both. Perhaps this is a result of a deep-seated, competitive need to obtain first breeding rights. We usually recommend that owners of two dogs get one male and one female.

Possessive Aggression

Some dogs, particularly those without strong leadership from their owner, can get abnormally attached to certain items. If these dogs are of the pushy, dominant type, it is likely they will become very protective of their favorite possessions. These dogs can become aggressive if a person or another dog comes close to their food bowls or most often something they have stolen. This type of aggression is usually learned rather than hereditary and therefore can be dealt with through behavior modification. The best way to prevent this type of aggression is to establish yourself as a strong leader right from the start, letting Bobo know that everything in the home is owned by you and that he gets to play with something only with your permission. For more information on this issue, refer to Chapter 5.

If you are present and you are the leader, your dog should understand that you have the ultimate say in the greeting procedure. Your dog should have confidence in you if you decide to greet a strange dog, because as the leader you would not jeopardize the safety of the pack.

Ideally, your dog should be socialized with other dogs from puppyhood on. This socialization begins in the litter, among the siblings. Again, it is very important for a puppy to stay with its litter until at least the *seventh week* of life; pups that leave the litter before this time have not had the opportunity to learn essential dog-to-dog social skills and often end up being fearful of or inept with other dogs later in life.

The following exercise works well in introducing two dogs that have a history of dog-to-dog aggression. It is not necessary to use this method with two playful, well-adjusted dogs.

1. Coordinate with a friend so that you can both walk your dogs at the same time. Meet on a corner away from either home so that there is no issue of territoriality involved. Do not allow your dogs to greet yet. Just begin walking next to each other, about 3 feet apart, with each dog on the left side of its owner (obedience classes teach how to walk a dog properly). Walk at a brisk, steady pace, and do not allow the dogs to greet yet. If they are being very uncooperative, just increase the distance between them until there is no chance that the dogs can come into contact. Try to think at this point that it is *your* walk, not your dog's, and that the dog is just along for the ride. The idea is that *you* are setting the parameters; you are saying to the dog, "First we do what *I* want, then we allow you to interact with your dog friend." Continue walking next to each other for a block or two.

2. Stop for a few seconds, say "okay," and let the dogs sniff each other. (If one or both dogs have a history of pronounced dog aggression, stop walking, but do not allow the dogs to come close to each other.) After a few seconds, begin walking again. Repeat this process every half block or so. Maintain a positive,

confident attitude throughout this procedure so that your dog does not sense fear on your part, a sure sign that you are not in charge.

3. After three or four of these quick greetings, stop and let the dogs sniff and posture for 20 or 30 seconds. Observe carefully, but remain calm and confident. The dogs will probably sniff each other's rears and posture for dominant positioning. This is a good opportunity for you to learn just how much dogs use their bodies to communicate and establish dominance. One dog may even try to mount the other at this point; you may also see marking behavior occur, which would involve urinating on objects. If no aggression occurs and the dogs have been relatively well behaved, separate them, have them sit, and reward each with a treat. Then return home, repeating several quick greetings between the dogs along the way. Repeat this entire procedure once each day for 2 weeks more or less as needed.

4. Once two dogs have been introduced in this controlled fashion, it should be possible to bring them to a fenced yard and let them loose to interact for brief periods of time. Bear in mind that the dog that considers the yard to be its territory may initially show some pushy behavior. This is normal; the dogs will work out their own little pecking order very quickly and adhere to it. If these two dogs showed pronounced aggressive tendencies toward each other during the walking exercises, however, it may not be advisable to let them loose in a yard, because a serious fight could ensue. (If this occurs, *never attempt to break it up yourself,* especially with two large dogs. Use a garden hose or a bucket of water to stop the aggression instead.)

By the time you have completed several sessions in the yard, the two dogs should have learned to tolerate each other quite well. You can then go through this entire exercise with another dog. The key to introducing two dogs is to begin on neutral territory and to do it gradually, with *you* dictating the terms from the very beginning until the end.

Many of you have nice, friendly dogs that don't need to go through this entire procedure. But if your dog is pushy and dominant and has learned to question your leadership status, we advise that you practice this exercise. Make sure that, throughout the procedure, you do not let Bobo see you get overly tense. Remember also to avoid overly tightening the lead, because that would tell Bobo that you are worried, something a leader shouldn't be.

Solution: Show Bobo Affection as an Earned Reward

Most persons are automatically drawn to a baby and play with it and shower it with attention. This is a normal human reaction and is beneficial to the child. The same reaction is usually directed toward puppies, which are arguably even cuter and more fun than babies. The problem is that human and canine psychology are not quite the same. When a human baby is spoiled, it can grow up to be obnoxious and selfish. When a puppy or young dog is constantly fawned over and made the center of attention, it too gradually develops an inflated sense of importance. The difference is that a dog that thinks it is the greatest can become a dominant, pushy animal capable of biting people.

Think again of the Alpha wolf. He occasionally pays attention to the juveniles in the pack, but more often than not he plays it cool and lets *them* fawn all over *him*. When one pack member gives its undying attention to another without expecting anything in return, it is because the giver recognizes the receiver as the dominant one of the pair. It is a simple signal of respect for authority. The dominant dog doesn't even have to accept attention from lower pack members if it doesn't want to. When you and your family coddle and shower your pup or adult dog with attention without asking for anything in return, therefore, the dog instinctively interprets this as *a sign of its dominance over you and the rest of the pack.*

This is not to say that you must always ignore your dog. To the contrary, interaction is good, provided it is initiated by you, and is *earned* by the dog. Many a dominant dog comes over to its owner, plops its head into his or her lap, and waits to be petted. This is a prime example of a dog initiating behavior, in this case asking a "subordinate" to groom it, much the way that the Alpha wolf does with his subordinates.

From now on, *make Bobo do something* for you before you pet or praise him. It can be something as simple as a sit, shake, or wait at a door. The idea is to get him to understand that *you* are now defining the terms of interaction, as a leader should. You are now in charge. There is nothing cold about this. It is simply the canine way, and after all, canine is the language your dog understands best.

Puppies too must obey this "earned praise" rule. If you want to praise and love your puppy, get it to do something for you. Simply calling little Bobo over to you will suffice. If he comes, praise him. Or tempt him into a sitting position by raising a treat over his head. If he sits, give him the treat and praise him all you want. The idea is *always to make the dog earn it.*

Bobo should be taught to understand that he is not the most important member of the pack. To the contrary, his pack status in the human hierarchy should be dead last. One way to accomplish this is to practice *ignoring* Bobo for periods of time, just as the Alpha wolf does with his subordinates when he has more pressing things to do.

Several times each day, tether Bobo to a doorknob on an 8- to 10-foot lead. Then, go about your business, in and out of the dog's field of view. (Don't actually leave him unattended, as he might accidentally get tangled up in the lead and hurt himself.) Completely ignore the dog for 15 to 20 minutes, even if he barks at you. If the barking becomes incessant, get a spray bottle, fill it with water, set it on a tight stream, and from 5 to 6 feet away, spray Bobo in the mouth while saying "no, quiet." After this period of time, approach Bobo, ask him to sit (if he knows how), then praise and release him. Only approach him when he is quiet, however; you don't want the dog to learn that barking gets you to come over and pay attention to him, even if your attention is negative. Dogs, like humans, prefer negative attention to no attention at all. Slowly, you can increase the tethering time to over an hour. This will help Bobo develop a sense of focus and patience. Try tethering Bobo during your dinnertime or when company comes over.

An alternative to tethering is using a travel crate. Some dogs attempt to chew through the lead or get tangled in it. Others simply feel more secure in a crate. If you use a crate for this exercise, place it where the dog can see you coming and going. First try the tethering technique, however; it allows Bobo to see you go about your business better than the crate technique. You want him to see that you have the right to do things without his participation.

If your dog is misbehaving, you can practice a "time-out." If Bobo begins barking at you to get your attention, for example, he might be in need of this exercise. Most owners yell at their dogs when they are barking. This doesn't work at all. It is interpreted by the dog as *you barking at it.* If you bark, why shouldn't it?

The time-out technique is the same as the ignoring exercise; put it in its crate, put the crate in a quiet place where he can't see anyone, then ignore it for 10 to 20 minutes. When the dog has calmed down, return to it, ask it to sit, then release and praise it. The object here is to teach your dog that if it misbehaves, it will be separated from the rest of the pack and ignored until it calms down and acts appropriately. This technique is nonconfrontational and plays on the dog's instinctive desire to be part of the pack. When it realizes that a certain behavior results in isolation, it will quickly learn to eliminate this behavior from its repertoire. The time-out should be done in a room away from the rest of the family, to teach Bobo that if he misbehaves, he gets isolated.

Solution: Tone Down Greeting and Departure Rituals

One of our clients has a pretty little Springer Spaniel named Sadie. The owner loved Sadie but unfortunately spoiled her to no end, creating a pushy, dominant mind-set in the dog. In addition, Sadie's owner always made a big emotional production out of leaving and coming home. As a result, Sadie began literally biting her owner in an attempt to prevent her from leaving for work in the morning. The owner had to resort to throwing cookies into the living room to distract Sadie so she could escape. Unfortunately, the treats served only to reinforce the bad behavior. We advised the owner to stop the frenetic greeting and departure rituals and to engage in some basic obedience techniques, including teaching Sadie to wait in the middle of the living room while the owner walked in and out of the front door. With the owner's husband holding Sadie's lead, the dog was physically incapable of performing her little biting technique. After about a month of consistent work, the owners finally broke Sadie of the habit.

People often go into an extremely emotion-packed mode on leaving or greeting their dogs. Creating a frenetic display like this gets your dog all worked up. "Oh Bobo, I missed you sooo much!!! Come here, come here, oh yesss, yessss!! Jump all over me!! Run around, even pee on me from the excitement!!" This is the wrong way to do it. You only serve to teach the dog to go nuts whenever you or anyone else comes in the home. Most people don't make such a fuss over greeting other *people*, so why do it with the dog? Often, owners feel guilty about leaving their dogs for the day so they create overly emotional greeting or departure rituals.

Instead, try something new. When you come home, ignore Bobo for a few minutes. Hang up your coat, check the mail, have a cup of coffee. Don't even look at the dog. If he is in the backyard, leave him out there for a bit. A dog that is used to a frenetic greeting from you will at first be confused and even get worse at first, but after 5 minutes or so will probably calm down and try to figure out what is going on. *That* is the time to *calmly and quietly* greet your dog. "Hi Bobo, how was your day?" That's it. Just as you would greet your spouse or teenager or neighbor. After 6 weeks of using this new method of greeting, you should see a difference in the way your dog reacts to people coming into your home. There will be much less jumping up and running around.

The same goes for departures. Don't walk up to your dog and say, "Oh Bobo, I'm leaving now and I'll really miss you, but don't worry, honey, I'll be back. . . ." It's unfair to the dog to do that because it makes him feel that you (the leader) are worried for some reason.

You create an atmosphere of concern in the dog. Instead, about 10 minutes before you leave, put your dog in the area where you would normally put him (yard, garage, living room, crate, kennel), go about your business, and then just leave. Don't create a melodramatic scene; just go.

By defusing high-energy greetings and departures, you will calm your dog down, reduce jumping and running around destruction while you are gone, and raise its confidence level. You will also make your home a calmer, easier place for all of you to live in.

Three

LEADERS MAINTAIN A DOMINANT POSTURE

The Alpha male lazily warms himself in the afternoon sun while two 4-month-old pups play-wrestle with each other close by. He watches them stalk, jump, and then chase each other around an old Douglas fir. Their play spills over into the Alpha's resting place, but they are having too much fun to notice. One of the pups, a male, suddenly decides to include the Alpha in the game. He jumps up at the Alpha's throat and mouth, biting and pawing at him, trying to goad him into play. The Alpha easily and calmly pins the pup down with one front paw, grabs him around the throat with his powerful jaws, and gently holds him, all the while growling softly. The pup rolls over on his back and, from that position, licks the Alpha's face. The Alpha returns the lick and walks away.

All the pups then run over to a juvenile female, who has been watching. She goes into play posture and goads the pups into chasing her around a large boulder. After a few minutes, she tires of the game and walks away from the pups, who try to keep the game going for a bit but then give up. They stop for a moment, wondering what to do next. Then, the dominant pup (the male that mouthed the Alpha) runs off quickly, the other one hot on his trail.

Being a wolf pack leader means acquiring and maintaining the highest position in the pack, not only in terms of social status but in terms of literal body placement as well. The leader must elevate himself above others to reinforce his status. If a challenger to his dominance comes into his space while he is resting, he will likely stand up to greet it instead of maintaining the more submissive down position. It is not that he necessarily senses a threat; rather, he sees this as the proper, traditional way for a leader to respond to the challenger. Walking up to the Queen of England and offering your hand, although a friendly gesture, would be considered by her to be an insult. Protocol demands a more respectful type of greeting procedure. If indeed she *did* shake your hand, she would lose face in front of her subjects for allowing such a breach of protocol. Her leadership would be diminished. A leader must obey the rules of leadership just as keenly as the rest of the pack.

When the spunky wolf pup began nipping at and teasing the Alpha male, the leader calmly and lovingly instructed the little upstart that his behavior, although amusing and admirable, was disrespectful and needed to change. He held him gently by the throat and stood over him, establishing a dominant position that the pup instinctively understood to mean, "Here's the way it is, kid; take note." The pup acknowledged this message by submissively licking the Alpha's face and turning belly-up. The Alpha then praised the pup by licking it back. Lesson learned, the spunky pup saved face in front of the other pup by running off and interacting with a young adult female of higher status than his own but far less than that of the Alpha.

The young female sensed the pup's desire to play and didn't wait for him to initiate. *She* began the chase game and had the pups chase *her*, the proper protocol when one canine is dominant over the other. The dominant animal *begins and ends the game* and also *sets the rules*. Finally tiring of the pups, the young female simply walked away and ignored them, leaving them to their own devices and allowing them to work out *their own pecking order* amongst themselves.

Posture and placement of your body can play a major role in establishing leadership with your dog. As the leader, you must be aware of how body-conscious your dog is. Canines are masters of body posture. It is an essential mode of communication between them. Eye contact, a form of body posturing, is also a powerful indicator of status; a subordinate canine cannot hold its gaze on a superior for long without risking some level of confrontation. When two canines are close in pack status and choose to vie with each other for dominance, one of the first things they do often is to enter into a staring contest. Normally, this activity is enough to decide the matter; the less dominant animal usually breaking off after a few seconds. If the competition between the two is not decided on this level, it will advance to physical displays of dominance, including strutting, mounting, false charges, leaning, and carefully orchestrated mouthing. Actual physical conflict is rare, but when it does occur, both parties usually exhibit preemptive signs of it, including stiffened hair on the neck and back, bared fangs, erect ears and tail, and slow, deliberate movement. Fights usually last only seconds and are the final arbiter of dominance.

Again, most dominance contests do not result in fighting; ritualistic positioning is normally enough to determine the pecking order. If it were not, the survival of the pack itself would be jeopardized. That is the prime advantage of the rigidly hierarchical structure of a canine pack; it is self-regulating and allows great cooperation among members. If fights resulting in injury were commonplace, the effectiveness of the group as well as the care and raising of the young would suffer greatly. Ultimately, the Alpha male is there to see to the unity and well-being of the pack so that it can function properly. He is an administrator more than he is a dictator.

Domestic dogs obey the same posturing rules as wolves. A dominant, pushy dog may lean on its owner; step on its owner's feet (not by accident); jump up on people; and in severe cases (often toward children), show mounting behavior. Dominant dogs may also be extremely mouthy and often attempt to attain a physically higher position than their owners, standing over them or constantly jumping into their lap without an invitation. This type of dog is only doing what it thinks it has the right and privilege to do, as the presumed leader of its pack.

By allowing this behavior to occur, the owner surrenders authority to the dog. To regain leadership, the owner must prevent the dog from exhibiting any of these dominant, physically intimidating behaviors.

Goal: To Maintain a Dominant Posture

A dog must not be allowed to use its body to control or alter its owner's behavior in any way. By regaining a dominant posture over your dog, you will teach it that you are higher in the pecking order than it thought you were. The solutions that follow give the owner nonconfrontational ways to do this.

Solution: Maintain an Upright Posture

Until they have completely won back the reins of leadership, owners of dominant, pushy dogs should never allow themselves to occupy a position that is physically lower than the dog's. Allowing the dog to stand above you while you lie on the floor is highly undesirable behavior. Even sitting on the floor with your dog standing next to you gives the wrong signal.

Try this experiment: Stand over Bobo and ask him to sit, and praise him if he does. Now, sit in a chair and ask him to sit. Did he? If he did, did it take longer for him to respond? Next, try sitting on the floor and again asking him to sit. What was his response this time? If you have a dominance problem with Bobo, chances are that he didn't sit this time but probably looked at you as if you were crazy. If you did get him to sit, next try lying on the floor and asking him to sit. Even well-adjusted dogs usually do not respond to the command this time. Why is this? The answer is simple; each time you physically lower your body in relation to the dog, you lower your status. The lower you go, the less clout you have.

    1. First, regularly practice elevating yourself over the dog. If the dog is standing in the middle of the room, for example, walk over and stand next to it. Don't pet it or even pay much

attention to it. Just stand upright above it. If your dog knows some obedience, ask it to sit or lie down with you standing next to it. This increases your status even more. Practice this simple change in posture often every day. When Bobo does sit or lie down, praise him and give him a treat.

2. If you are sitting in a sofa or on a chair and your dog knows the "lie down" command, have it lie down next to you. A dog that stands next to a sitting person is more or less on equal footing. By lowering it into a "down," you can remedy that. If Bobo doesn't know "down," you can ask him to sit, which is a slightly less dominant posture than standing. If Bobo knows no obedience at all, at least attempt to sit with your body above him.

Also try asking Bobo to sit when he is not looking at you and when there are distractions present. Keep his 8- to 10-foot lead on during this practice, and require him to pay attention. If he simply refuses to sit or focus on you, tether him to a doorknob for half an hour, ignore him, and then try it again.

3. Do not allow Bobo to rest in an area that allows him to be higher than your position. For example, a dominant dog should not be allowed to lie on the top of a flight of steps and watch you down below. This is an overt signal of dominance. Bobo can just as easily rest on the same floor as you, so deny him access to this elevated position when you are below. Clip Bobo's 8- to 10-foot lead on him and physically move him to a more desirable area. If he continues to get up and return to the higher area, simply move him again and then tether the lead to something, preventing him from returning to his dominant perch. Denying Bobo access to this area for at least 6 to 8 weeks should break the habit.

Solution: Prevent Jumping Up, Leaning, Stepping on Your Feet, or Mouthing

A dominant dog may exhibit any or all of these obnoxious, controlling behaviors. All of them point to a dog that does not know its place. The following solutions are designed to reduce or eliminate these bad behaviors.

JUMPING UP

Dogs jump up onto people for many reasons. This bad habit probably started when Bobo was just a puppy. He was cute and small, and when you came home from a hard day's work, you were so happy to see him that you probably encouraged him to leap up at you. He licked your face and yipped his approval, and you rewarded the behavior by petting and verbally praising him. Then Bobo started to grow, and it ceased to be so cute when this 40- or 50-pound dog continued to throw itself at you whenever it wanted to. Have you noticed, perhaps, that your friends don't come over as often, now that little Bobo isn't so little anymore? Do you blame them? There is nothing more obnoxious than having a dog put its muddy paws all over your clean suit or dress.

Many dominant, pushy dogs jump on people to get their attention. "Pet me! Hey! Look at me!" Jumping is also a way of physically controlling others whom Bobo feels need to be controlled. Sometimes, although rarely, jumping can even be a symptom of aggression. If Bobo has learned to behave in this way, however, he can *unlearn* it. If your dog jumps up on you, there is a fairly simple, nonconfrontational way of stopping the behavior.

1. Walk up to Bobo and pet him on the head. If he jumps up on you, don't yell or get angry. Instead, firmly hold his front paws and *don't let go*. While doing this, talk to the dog in a calm voice. After a few moments, Bobo is going to say, "Okay that's enough, let go now." He will begin trying to pull his feet away. After a bit longer, Bobo will begin to get annoyed and may mouth your hands in a display of dominant frustration. After about 10 seconds, let go of its paws and say "off." When Bobo's front paws touch the floor, say "good off." In this way, you make it clear to him that having all four feet on the ground is a desirable thing.

2. Call Bobo back over and attempt to get him to jump up on you again. If he does, repeat Step 1. After two rounds of this, almost any dog will learn not to jump on you again.
3. Work this technique two times each day for a week or so and then periodically if necessary. All members of the family should work this, provided they are strong enough to hold the dog's paws.

If Bobo is just too excitable to keep himself from jumping all over your friend, try *standing* on the lead so that there isn't enough slack to allow him to jump. If he tries to jump, the lead will stop him, provided your foot is securely positioned on the lead. If your dog is aggressive, do not do this.

JUMPING ON GUESTS

If Bobo likes to dominate guests by jumping on them when they come over, try this solution (this will also work for children in the family):

1. Call a friend and ask him or her to come over at a specific time. Tell the friend to knock and then just come in. Also instruct your friend to be calm and almost indifferent to Bobo. At no time should he or she try to get Bobo all worked up and excited.
2. Before your friend arrives, clip Bobo's lead onto his collar and hold onto the end of it.
3. When your friend comes in, observe the dog. If Bobo attempts to jump up, say *no* and walk him away from your friend. Then, ask Bobo to sit (assuming he knows how). Praise him for sitting, and then have your friend approach. Each time Bobo jumps, say *no* and walk him away, denying him the privilege of greeting your friend.
4. If you cannot hold him because he is too strong and active, tie him to something secure before you open the door. When he calms down your friend can now go pet him. If he gets worked

up again, walk away until he calms down. Continue this until he understands what he is getting praised for.

Eventually, Bobo will learn that when he *doesn't* jump, he gets rewarded. In this case, the reward is being greeted and petted by your friend. It may take half a dozen attempts, but Bobo will catch on. Ideally, Bobo should learn that sitting politely is the proper position in which to greet people. If Bobo is sitting, he can't be jumping.

JUMPING INTO YOUR LAP

If you desire to have your small dog jump up into your lap while you are on the sofa, it should be *by invitation only*, on your terms. If the dog has a serious dominance problem, which many small dogs do because of undue spoiling, we recommend you do not allow it up on you at all until you have firmly established your leadership.

1. Clip Bobo's lead onto his collar, and sit down on the sofa.
2. If Bobo immediately jumps up on you or the sofa, say *no*, grab hold of the lead, and physically remove Bobo from the sofa. Try not to get off the sofa when you do this; you do not want Bobo to learn that he can manipulate your movements in any way. If you must get up, move him away from you and sit down again.
3. Repeat this technique as many times as necessary to show Bobo that jumping up is not proper behavior.
4. If necessary, tether Bobo to a doorknob within sight of the sofa, and sit down and read the newspaper. Ignore him if he barks, but if the barking gets out of hand, spray him with water *from where you are sitting*.
5. Once Bobo clearly understands that he cannot jump up on you or the sofa whenever he wants to, you can, if you desire, call him up onto the sofa by saying "up." Then, when you want him off, say "off," and remove him from the sofa by using the lead. Praise him when he is on the floor. Eventually Bobo will learn the "up" and "off" commands, and he should understand that he is allowed up on you or the furniture *by invitation only*.

LEANING OR STEPPING ON YOUR FEET

Last year we received a call from a teenage boy regarding a problem that his grandmother was having with her 8-year-old English Bulldog, Bob. We asked the boy why his grandmother wasn't calling. His reply was that she didn't think there was a problem. It seemed that when Dottie (the grandmother) would settle down into her easy chair after dinner to watch television, Bob would lie on top of her feet and go to sleep. If Dottie tried to get up, Bob would bite her feet, often hard enough to draw blood. The grandson told us that Dottie was often forced by Bob to spend hours in the chair and was able to get up only when Bob woke up and wandered off. More than once, she ended up spending the night in the chair.

We were amazed at the level of dominance Bob had attained over Dottie and thought of what a perfect example it was of a dog maintaining a dominant posture over its owner. We told the caring grandson to have Dottie give us a call, but she never did. Seemingly, she enjoyed having her feet warmed *and* bitten by Bob.

A dominant dog may make a habit of leaning on you and stepping on your feet. Although Bobo loves you, don't mistake this behavior for affection. Both are ways of controlling and dominating you with his body. Dogs use their bodies to control other dogs all the time. As the leader, you can't afford to play into this behavior. If you are sitting on the sofa and Bobo comes over and leans his big old body on you, the last thing you should do is absentmindedly reach down and pet him. By doing so, you reward the pushy behavior and tell Bobo that it's okay to dominate you.

If Bobo comes over and leans his big body into you or steps on you, immediately say "no, off," and then walk away. Let him realize that his attempts to dominate you physically will result in his being ostracized. When Bobo comes over and greets you honorably, you can pet and praise him. Be consistent with this technique, and you should see a change in a few weeks. If he is insistent about leaning into you or stepping on you, simply tether him to a doorknob across the room and ignore him for a little while. By doing so, you tell him that you are not willing to let him control you anymore.

MOUTHING

When puppies are among their littermates, they do lots of mouthing and play-biting. An essential behavior at this age, it helps establish their pecking order and teaches them how hard they can bite before causing pain (this gauging of bite strength is called bite inhibition). It takes them a while to learn what hurts and what doesn't. A dog that is constantly hurting other pack members would cause great turmoil and would ultimately be ostracized or severely corrected.

When a pup comes home with you, therefore, it has a history of mouthing behind it. Your family is a new litter, so it instinctively thinks it has the right to mouth and play-bite again. You and your family must discourage this behavior; it is not at all appropriate because, as the lowest member of the pack, it shouldn't have the right to mouth anyone. Ideally, a pup should learn not to mouth you by the time it is 12 to 14 weeks old. Following are several methods you can use to discourage mouthing by a pup or an adult dog:

1. The moment your pup or adult Bobo mouths you, let out a loud "owww!" This sound will momentarily surprise him and make him aware that he has caused you pain. This is exactly how pups in the litter learn that they are biting a sibling too forcibly. Then, offer your open palm to Bobo, encouraging him to lick instead of bite. This method will work well if the biting is not too serious a problem, provided you and your entire family practice it consistently. This technique will not work with a dog that has a serious biting problem.

2. Another effective technique is to isolate Bobo whenever he puts his mouth on a human. First, make sure his lead is clipped onto his collar. As soon as he mouths someone, tell him "no bite," tether him to a doorknob, and ignore him for at least 10 minutes. Ignore any barking or tantrums, and return to him *only when he is quiet even if that takes longer than 10 minutes.* Repeat this technique whenever any mouthing occurs. Bobo should quickly learn to associate the mouthing with the time-out and adjust his behavior accordingly.

3. Another simple technique that can help is the use of a spray bottle. Fill a plant sprayer with water, adjust it to a tight stream, and as soon as Bobo mouths you, spray him right in the kisser while saying "no bite." It helps to have several sprayers located throughout the home so that you can get to one quickly. The spraying of Bobo needs to occur during or as close to the mouthing incident as possible for it to have any behavioral effect.

If Bobo has a serious mouthing or biting problem that involves breaking of the skin or overtly using his teeth to control the behavior of others, we *strongly advise you to see a canine behaviorist* for help. Baring of the teeth is indicative of *serious aggression* and not mere dominance. Aggression of this type can be made worse by the well-meaning attempts of most owners. Let a pro help.

Solution: Avoid Playing Bad Games with Your Dog

Playtime isn't just playtime to your dog. It is also a way of working out its place in the pecking order. Watch two dogs cavorting in a yard. The dominant one almost never chases but rather is chased. It also begins the game, and when it tires of it, it ends it. As the dominant dog, it sets the terms of engagement. If it didn't, the other dog would take it as a sign of weakness and challenge its leadership.

Even leaders desire play. The difference is that leaders begin and end the play and determine the rules. When you play with Bobo, you must set the terms of engagement and never allow him to assert himself against you or compete on an even footing. If Bobo, a subordinate, is allowed to win at play-wrestling with you, for example, you will lose status in his eyes because you let him learn that his strength is equal to or greater than yours. If human parents allow their child to win every game of tic-tac-toe, that child will develop an unrealistic, inflated sense of importance and will eventually feel superior to the parents. When he or she gets into the real world, however, things will be a whole lot different. The leader of the pack must retain a sense of authority by never allowing other pack members to overpower him, even at play.

As leader, you must mimic this attitude with Bobo. Only play games that avoid letting him pit his strength and speed against yours. You will lose out, and Bobo will interpret your showing as poor leadership. The following are some games that can damage your status as leader:

TUG-OF-WAR

Few games erode an owner's leadership more than this one. When you and Bobo play tug-of-war, you say to him, "Yes, Bobo, you are as strong as I am and often stronger." Not only do owners play this game too often, they let their dogs *win* at it, a classic mistake that subverts their leadership "big time." A dominant, pushy dog should never play this game with its owner, especially if it is of an inherently dominant breed such as a Rottweiler, German Shepherd, or Bullmastiff. The only exception to this rule is if you have a dog that is severely lacking in confidence and needs to be lifted up a few pegs. Playing tug-of-war can help accomplish that.

Never let your children play tug-of-war with Bobo, no matter how much they want to. Children have a hard enough time establishing leadership as it is. They don't need to send additional messages to Bobo that they are weak or inferior in any way.

CHASE GAMES

Last year, the owner of a beautiful 3-year-old Shetland Sheepdog came to us for help in getting her dog to stop chasing after and biting joggers. She lived right next to a well-used bicycle and running path. Alex easily jumped the 4-foot fence that separated him from the path and had great fun terrorizing morning joggers. He wasn't actually being aggressive; rather, he was expressing a combination of territorial concerns and herding drive. Shetland Sheepdogs (or Shelties) were bred to be herders and naturally want to herd animals, children, and even joggers running by. In addition, any dog will become protective when seeing strangers running toward its territory.

After quizzing Alex's owner on the dog's history and environment, we discovered several shortcomings that were playing into the undesirable behavior. First, the owner's two young children regularly played chase games with Alex in the yard when they got home from school. This encouraged Alex to think that chasing humans was an acceptable game to play and also taught him that humans were okay to herd, just as sheep are. After more questioning, we also learned that Alex tended to nip at the children's heels during the chasing, a common technique used by herding dogs to affect the sheep's direction. So Alex's owners inadvertently taught him that it was okay to chase and nip at humans.

The second big mistake that the owner made was to allow Alex visual access to the jogging/bike path. Alex spent all day seeing these strangers rushing right by his backyard and got frustrated at not being able to do anything about it. After all, it was his yard, and in his mind, these strangers were trying to invade it. Eventually, it became too much for him; he learned that he could vault the 4-foot chain-link fence and give these strangers a run for their money.

The solution to the problem was straightforward. First, the chase games with the children had to stop completely to discontinue reinforcing the idea that it's okay to chase humans. Second, Alex could no longer be kept in a location that allowed visual access to the busy path. We suggested that he be allowed to stay in the home instead. Because of his excellent house-training habits, this posed no problem at all. For the times when Alex was in the yard, we recommended a higher fence, of a design that did not allow Alex to see through. Last, we enrolled Alex and his owner in a basic obedience class to try to get him thinking about cause and effect and to build the owner's leadership skills. Within 3 months, the problem disappeared.

Leaders don't chase. Alex's owners learned that the hard way. Owners that run after their dogs are doing exactly what subordinates do with the Alpha leader. By chasing Bobo, you teach him that *you can't catch him.* He's got four legs to your two, and there is no way you'll defeat him. This is a prime example of how owners lose leadership to their dogs.

Instead, get Bobo to come to you. Praise him when he runs toward you, and ignore him when he attempts to goad you into chasing him. If you have two dogs, by all means allow them to chase each other to work out their own pecking order. Don't allow any dog, however, to learn that it is faster and more agile than you. Humans are humbled by the speed and strength of most animals. All we have going for us is our brains.

WRESTLING

Many of our clients have dominant, nippy dogs that learned to be this way in part because of inappropriate wrestling games played from the time their dogs were puppies. We had one client whose children constantly wrestled with the family dog, a male Bullmastiff named Rudy. When Rudy was a pup, he was adorable. The 10- and 12-year-old boys couldn't play with him enough, and they regularly wrestled with him as soon as they got home from school. By the time Rudy was 10 months old, however, he had turned into a 130-pound ball of muscle. To compound the problem, his owners refused to neuter him. The combination of breed temperament, surging hormones, and improper wrestling games added up to create an extremely dominant dog that thought he could do no wrong. Eventually, during a heated bout of wrestling, he bit the 10-year-old on the upper arm, breaking the skin and sending the boy screaming to his mother.

When the family came to us the next day, we made it clear to them just what they had done wrong. First, the choice of such a strong, dominant, territorial breed was not the best one for a family with children. That said, we concentrated on things they could do to prevent the biting from occurring again. The wrestling *absolutely had to stop* so that Rudy would not continue to think that humans were weak little playthings to be tossed around and dominated. In addition, the family needed to take a basic obedience course and bring the children to the class so that they too could learn how to gain leadership over Rudy.

Because it is a prime way that Bobo can learn to question your authority, wrestling should be curtailed or eliminated, particularly in the case of a dominant dog that doesn't recognize you as leader. Again, the dog is stronger and faster than you and will use its mouth during this type of strength contest. You will be teaching Bobo that he is stronger and that he can put his mouth on you.

Children like to wrestle with dogs. Unfortunately, they are the last ones who should be doing this. They are small to start with, and their size is interpreted by Bobo as meaning they are "low on the totem pole." When he wrestles children, Bobo plainly sees their weaknesses and develops a sense of dominion over them. A dog that feels superior to children will not think twice about biting one if the child gets out of hand. Don't wrestle with a shy, withdrawn dog, either. It might interpret the physical contention as punishment or anger, and you might end up making the dog worry even more.

Solution: Play Good Games with Your Dog

What games *can* you play with Bobo? Here are some good ones that won't compromise your status as leader.

FETCH

This game not only is fun for Bobo and you, it also teaches him to retrieve a toy and bring it back to you, the leader. The game supports your status and teaches Bobo to come to you.

Ideally you should begin the fetch when Bobo is a puppy, although it isn't crucial to do that. Find a toy that he loves; it could be a ball, stick, Frisbee, rubber bumper (used by hunters to teach retrieving to their dogs), or anything else Bobo is crazy for. First, get him excited about playing with it in a room, perhaps tantalizing him with it a bit. Then, toss it just a foot or two and encourage him to go get it. When he does, happily encourage him to come back to you with the toy. If he does, praise him liberally, before taking the toy away. If he doesn't come back to you, attach a 20- to 30-foot lead to him and guide him back to you. Work the fetch a few times, then *put the toy away*. Make sure that you stop the game when he is still eager to continue. If you let him lose interest, he won't be quite as excited to play next time. Bobo should see this toy only when you play fetch. If he had constant access to the toy, he would eventually get bored with it. Gradually lengthen the distance as well as the number of times you throw the toy for Bobo. Also, remember that you, the leader, begin and end all games.

Some dogs get in trouble with their owners for stealing items in the home such as socks or shoes. These dogs may not want to play fetch, because they have been reprimanded in the past for picking things up in their mouths. If this is the case, don't push the fetch. Even these dogs can in time come to discriminate between allowable play toys and your personal items. You have to have patience with your dog and praise him when he is doing the right thing.

FLYBALL

The game of flyball is a variation of fetch. A flyball machine is basically a small catapult device that launches a tennis ball into the air the moment a dog steps on a triggering pedal mounted on the front. The dog is usually taught to sit and wait about 20 feet away from the flyball machine while the owner "loads" it with a tennis ball. When the command is given, the dog runs up to the machine and steps on the release pedal, launching the ball up into the air above the dog's head. The dog learns to leap up at just the right moment to catch the ball and then returns to the starting point (or wherever else the owner decides it should return to).

If you intend to teach Bobo to play flyball, you must first teach him to catch a tennis ball in his mouth. Start teaching him to catch pieces of popcorn first. Have him sit, and from 2 or 3 feet away, toss pieces of popcorn at his mouth. At first he won't have the timing or coordination down properly. Keep trying. He will eventually figure it out. Once he can catch popcorn, you can try dog cookies. Then, move on to a tennis ball, first throwing it to him from only 3 or 4 feet away and gradually increasing the distance.

Flyball clubs have sprung up across the country, holding relay competitions between teams of dogs. It's great fun and teaches the dog to improve its agility.

"ROUND-ROBIN" RECALL

This simple game will improve Bobo's desire to come to you and is plenty of fun to boot. Three or four family members or friends should spread themselves out so that they are located on the corners of a triangle or square, about 10 to 15 feet from each other. One person should have Bobo in front of him or her, and all should have some small treats in their pockets.

One person calls Bobo enthusiastically and rewards him with a treat and lots of praise when he comes. Then, another person calls him and repeats the reward, then another and another, quickly, so that Bobo has to go round and round the shape from person to person, in an excited, happy state. You can gradually enlarge the shape until Bobo is coming to each person over a distance of 30 or 40 feet. Also begin calling him in a random order so that you can be sure he is truly listening and not just anticipating. This game is a great way to perfect the "come" command, one of the most important and potentially lifesaving commands Bobo will ever learn.

AGILITY AND TRICKS

Any trick you teach Bobo, be it "shake" or "roll over," is fun for him and teaches him to think. Teaching tricks is also a positive experience for you and can only help bolster your position as leader. Dogs like learning tricks much more than learning basic obedience. It is like the difference in motivation between learning algebra and learning soccer for a teenager. Learning tricks can also boost a dog's confidence level. Teaching agility tricks to Bobo, such as jumping over an obstacle or going through a tunnel, can be exciting for him as well as great exercise. It also helps build a better, more trusting relationship between the two of you. Fearful or timid dogs can have their confidence levels greatly increased by learning tricks.

There are many books and videotapes on the market that can help get you started teaching Bobo tricks. Realize, however, that there is no one way to teach a trick. You can make up your own methods. Whatever works, works. Just remember that when teaching Bobo tricks, you should use absolutely no negative reinforcement. Use positive methods only. A list of standard tricks that you might teach Bobo follows:

- Shake
- Speak
- Roll over
- Spin
- Beg
- Play dead
- Find it
- Over (a jump)
- Wave
- Bring the leash

If you are interested in competition agility (teaching Bobo to run a timed obstacle course), you can locate a canine agility club in your area by contacting your vet, a local shelter, or any local dog trainer. Another option would be to locate and join a tracking club. Bobo could learn to use his strongest sense, that of smell, to locate objects or persons over long distances. To see a dog track and locate an item after a prolonged search is a rewarding experience for most owners and one that fosters a climate of mutual respect and love.

Four

LEADERS GO FIRST

The pack was on the move, looking for food. They had scented the recent passage of a group of mule deer, but the scent was weakened by a late storm that deposited 6 inches of new snow in the valley. Three days had passed since the last kill, and the Alpha knew he needed to lead his pack to something soon.

The end of the valley narrowed into a tight gorge with high, eroded sandstone walls. The trees here were sparse, mostly larch and a few young aspens. Most of the ground was choked with thick stands of wild blackberries and dwarf pines. The Alpha led the pack along a slim trail that wound through the thorny blackberry bushes and headed for a narrow pass regularly used by deer to enter and exit the valley. It was tight going. The pack had to travel single file to avoid getting pricked by thorns. The Alpha went first, closely followed by his mate and their 5-month-old pups, a male and a female. Behind them were two subordinate males, three year-old females, and an older lone female who had been loosely accepted by the pack a week before.

Once out through the pass, the Alpha immediately picked up the scent of droppings close to the trail. He trotted over to a grassy area near a small pool of water and found fresh deer droppings, no more than 10 minutes old. Each wolf in turn sniffed at the droppings, then followed on, excited and confident that soon their leader would locate the deer.

One of the subordinate males picked up the scent of a female mule deer in heat and, in his excitement, bounded ahead of the pack. The Alpha was not pleased with this; the young male was not as experienced at tracking and could very well spook the deer, ruining the chances for a successful hunt. He quickly and silently snapped out at the young male *as he went by, then forced him off the trail into some loose sandstone scree. The Alpha then jogged back to the head of the procession and continued tracking the female mule deer, who was now very close. The young male fell back into the procession, somewhat embarrassed but otherwise no worse for the incident.*

After they fed on the old female mule deer, the wolves rested and groomed each other. The young male, sleepy from the large meal, quietly lay down a few yards from the Alpha. The leader rose, walked over to the young male, and stood next to him, pawing slightly at the ground. They licked each other's faces and joined the rest of the pack for a well-earned sleep.

The leader of the wolf pack, by definition, goes first. He must go first, because he is the best qualified to do so. He has the experience, the wisdom, and the know-how to deal with any unforeseen circumstances that might arise. It is his duty to go first, in case danger presents itself. It is, after all, his responsibility to see that his pack is safe, well fed, and healthy. Being the first in line or the first to investigate something is also the Alpha leader's privilege and a signal to the others that here is a wolf of importance, a wolf to be respected. Caesar before the troops, so to speak.

As the wolf pack made its way down the narrow pathway, it naturally organized itself according to the existing pecking order, with the two Alphas and their pups out in front, followed by the subordinate males and females and, finally, an older lone female who only recently had been accepted into the pack. She had the least status and was pretty much thankful for the company and the help in hunting. Each wolf instinctively knew exactly where it should be in relation to the others. Even when sniffing at the droppings, they knew to do it in order of importance.

When the scent of the female mule deer became apparent, however, the young male temporarily lost his head and excitedly ran out ahead of his leader. This act could not be tolerated. Having less hunting and tracking experience, the youngster might have spooked the deer and doomed the pack to another hungry night. The Alpha leader plainly could not allow this to occur, so he quickly and efficiently disciplined the young male, preventing him from ruining their chances of success. The young male quickly learned his lesson and fell back into his proper place, with no hard feelings. After the kill and the much-needed feeding, the Alpha made a point of socializing with the young male to show him that there was no animosity between them and that he had in the end redeemed himself by helping to bring down the deer. The leader in this way showed that he held no grudge whatsoever and was content with their relationship.

Bobo understands and obeys the same rules that the wolves in the preceding scenario do. He knows that whoever goes first is the leader, literally. Study a small pack of dogs and watch the animals closely when they enter and exit a room. Odds are that the same dog goes out and comes in first and that the order remains the same. Those dogs arrange themselves according to their pecking order and stick to it pretty consistently.

Most owners are not aware of the "leaders go first" rule. Observe any person walking down the street with his or her dog; chances are the dog is way out ahead, pulling its hapless master down the street, oblivious to everything except its own immediate concerns. "Get me to the park! Let's go see my friend Fido! Hurry up!" This is what the dominant, pushy dog is thinking when it hurdles down the street with its subordinate owner in tow.

A few years ago, we had a client come to us for help in getting her 3-year-old male Newfoundland, Bart, to stop pulling her all over the place during walks. Bart was friendly and affectionate with everyone and loved his owner, a middle-aged single woman barely 5 feet in high heels, who weighed under a hundred pounds. Bart, on the other hand, weighed about 140 pounds and was over 6 feet tall when standing on his hind legs. His owner was simply outmatched physically in every department.

To compound matters, Bart's owner had spoiled him badly from puppyhood on. She let him sleep with her, fed him food from her plate, let him knock her down and sit on her, and allowed him to mouth her constantly, thinking the little nips were "love bites." Bart's owner in fact did everything she possibly could to teach him that *he* was the leader, short of giving him the keys to the car (and he did try to sit on her lap while she drove).

Every morning since puppyhood, Bart and his owner would walk down to the lake, and he would go for a swim, something that Newfoundlands love to do. Each day Bart got bigger and stronger, and he pulled harder and harder on the lead because he knew that at the end of the walk, the cool clear lake awaited. That was his reward. And each day his owner had a harder and harder time trying to hold on. She was afraid to let go for fear that Bart would get hit by a car. One day, as they neared the lake, Bart saw that a few geese were swimming close to shore. One of his favorite games was to chase them in the water; he'd almost caught one once. As soon as he saw the geese, he took off as fast as he could, with his tiny owner holding onto the lead for dear life, still worried that Bart might be struck by a car. She finally fell, but she still wouldn't let go. Bart literally dragged her all the way down to the lake and into the water before she finally let go of the lead.

Bart had been given no rules to live by and no boundaries. His owner had surrendered total control to him; in Bart's eyes, she was merely a beloved subordinate. Although he cared for her, he certainly did not take her seriously, and he wouldn't have hesitated to hurt her again to fulfill some need of his own. She came to us the next day to get our help in controlling Bart. When we saw her, we were amazed; she was covered with bandages from head to toe, and she was crying because she thought we would recommend euthanasia. Even though she was substantially injured, she was still thinking of "poor" Bart, whom she loved so much.

This was a classic example of a dog being in charge of its owner, and we knew we needed to help this woman before she got pulled out into the middle of rush hour traffic by her beloved Bart. First, we recommended that Bart stay with us for 2 weeks to receive some long-delayed basic obedience training. We taught him all the basics, but above all, we had to teach him to accept leadership and to *think*. Most dogs are not taught to think through things, and instead, they simply *react to stimuli* in an almost autonomic sense. Bart was guilty of this. If he saw a goose, he would simply take off after it, not thinking of the consequences of perhaps getting hit by a car or hurting his owner.

The most pressing obedience issue with Bart, apart from lowering his status and turning his brain on, was getting him to stop pulling out ahead on the lead. We wanted him to walk nicely right next to us, on the left side, with the lead *loose* instead of taut as a bowstring. We quickly got him to stop the pulling through the use of leash corrections; each time Bart rushed out ahead, we popped the lead sharply, told him "no, don't pull," then abruptly turned and walked in the opposite direction, repeating the procedure as many times as necessary until he realized that when he walked next to us, he did not get a correction but, instead, praise. Our concern, however, was that Bart's owner would not be emotionally or physically capable of administering the types of corrections necessary to stop Bart from pulling her. She was, in his eyes, truly submissive.

To solve the pulling problem for her, we resorted to using a piece of equipment known as a "head collar," a device similar in design and function to the halter on a horse. It fits over the dog's muzzle and has a metal ring that hangs down directly underneath the dog's chin. The lead clips to this ring, and when taken for a walk, the dog simply *cannot* pull without being easily stopped with only slight pressure from the owner. The head collar works on the principle that if you can control the head of the animal, you automatically control the body, no matter how big it is. This is how horses are controlled. Without a halter, there would be no possibility of leading and controlling a thousand-pound animal. Bart might as well have been a horse to his owner, so we decided to have her use the head collar. It also had the advantage of not seeming as confrontational as a lead connected to a choke chain or prong collar.

Because Bart's owner had ridden horses, she instantly understood how the head collar would work and that it was not harmful. After working with her for several sessions, Bart's owner learned how to use the head collar successfully to stop him from dragging her all over the countryside. Once this was accomplished, she could easily work Bart on his obedience and thereby gain leadership in his eyes.

All dogs, be they big or small, need to learn not to get out ahead of their owners and pull on the lead. There are several reasons for this. First and foremost, in the dog world, leaders *lead*. Period. If you allow Bobo to get out in front and pull you down the street, you are surrendering leadership to him and telling him that you'd rather have *him* deal with any unexpected events that pop up, such as a stray dog or a jogger running by. You are in effect taking a backseat and letting *him* drive and navigate. Second, it is unsafe to let Bobo get out ahead and call all the shots. Remember that he has the mind of a 2-year-old child and may not be able to determine whether he is walking into a potentially dangerous situation. As leader, *you* should be determining that, not him. Dogs that hurriedly pull their owners down the street can also, as seen with Bart, injure their owners by pulling them down to the ground, through brambles, or out into a busy city street. Many dogs, over time, injure their own tracheas by pulling so hard. This is especially true of small dogs, whose necks are not nearly as strong as those of larger dogs.

Another concern is the mind-set that is created in a dog at the end of a constantly taut lead. When Bobo is pulling with all his might, straining to get down to the park or his favorite tree, he isn't thinking at all but mindlessly anticipating. A taut lead teaches Bobo that he doesn't have to pay attention to where you are or what you are doing; he knows exactly where you are, precisely because *of* the pressure on the lead. If the lead were loose, he'd be forced to pay more attention to just where you were; this would cause him to focus and think more, two of the primary goals that you need to achieve with him.

A taut lead can also be a signal to Bobo that you are nervous about something. For instance, if you are walking him down the street at night and up ahead you see a group of questionable-looking characters coming toward you, chances are you will instinctively get a firmer, tighter grip on the lead, significantly increasing the level of tension. Bobo will interpret this as fear or apprehension on your part. You, his supposed leader and protector, are telegraphing your concern right down the taut lead and into him. This has the effect of making him feel insecure and fearful. By increasing leash pressure, therefore, you can, under the right circumstances, create a worrisome mind-set in Bobo, possibly leading to fear aggression or other undesirable behaviors. At the very least, it will reduce his confidence level.

In addition, excess manipulation of the lead can bring out other latent aggressive behaviors in Bobo. When dogs are trained to be attack or protection dogs, one way that a trainer can incite a dog to show aggression toward a subject is by keeping a very taut lead while using tense vocal cues. This tactic tends to enrage or "fire up" the dog; when finally released, the dog attacks. Owners that keep a taut lead with their dogs can also cause a heightened level of aggression in their dogs. Allowing Bobo to pull out ahead of you on a taut lead not only reduces your status as leader, therefore, but creates other undesirable behaviors as well.

Another arena where leadership is won or lost is at the front or back door to the home. Most dogs simply bound out or in the door ahead of their owners. By allowing this to happen, you tell Bobo in no uncertain terms that he is the leader and you are the subordinate. In this chapter, we teach you how to get Bobo to wait at the door until you have stepped out. By doing so, you will gain precious status points in Bobo's eyes.

This chapter also deals with another area that often causes owners much grief: getting Bobo to come to you when called. Most dogs, because they lack the proper respect for their owners, simply won't come when called. This causes many owners to resort to chasing their pets all over the place, resulting in an even further degradation of leadership. We show you how to avoid having to chase Bobo around by teaching him to come to you reliably every time.

Goal: To Show Bobo That You, the Leader, Always Go First

Solution: Teach Bobo to Walk by Your Side on a Loose Lead

Although we sometimes use corrections with a lead and training collar when modifying improper behaviors, we have decided largely to avoid teaching the use of corrections in the book, opting instead for less confrontational methods. Again, the object of this book is to help you gain, or regain, leadership over Bobo by practicing simple, nonconfrontational exercises. To teach Bobo not to get out ahead and pull on a lead, you will need two pieces of equipment. One is a strong 6-foot walking lead, separate from the 8- to 10-foot one used in the home. The other is the head collar, which is available at most good pet shops in many sizes. It comes with explicit instructions regarding how to fit it properly to Bobo. We feel that using the head collar is the quickest and least confrontational way to get a dominant pushy dog to walk next to you on a loose lead, instead of incessantly pulling out ahead. If your dog can't use a head collar, there are also some harnesses specially made for no pulling. They work very well.

First, go to the pet store and purchase a head collar device to fit Bobo. If you are unsure of what size to buy, refer to the packaging. It will normally match each size head collar to a specific size *and breed* of dog. The breed is as important a factor as the size of the dog, because some breeds have very short or long muzzles that may require you to go up or down a size to achieve a proper fit. For example, a Boxer, although considered a fairly large dog, may end up wearing a head collar that fits a smaller breed, such as a Brittany, which weighs on average 20 pounds less than a Boxer but has a longer muzzle. If you are still unsure after reading the sizing instructions on the package, consult an employee of the store; he or she has probably sold dozens of head collars and will be able to recommend the proper size. Generally, dogs such as Miniature Poodles, Pugs, or Whippets take an extra small; Beagles, Cocker Spaniels, and American Eskimos a small; Labrador Retrievers, Standard Poodles, and Golden Retrievers a medium; German Shepherds, Rottweilers, and Pit Bulls a large; and Newfoundlands, Saint Bernards, and Great Danes an extra large.

The most difficult step in using a head collar is getting Bobo used to wearing it. It fits over Bobo's muzzle and is secured in place by a collar that is held high up behind the neck, close to the ears. (See the manufacturer's instructions for proper fitting.) Bobo may object at first to having something rubbing up against the top of his muzzle; he will probably paw at it, trying to get it off. The first step in the process, therefore, is for you to desensitize Bobo to having it on. First, call him over to you. Make him sit, and give him a treat. Praise him lavishly, then very casually slip the head collar on over his muzzle and secure it around his upper neck, just behind the ears. At this point, before he has a chance to object, give him another treat (the head collar will not interfere with his eating or drinking), and praise him enough to keep his mind off the head collar. Then, remove the collar, and give him another treat. Repeat this procedure several times within a few hours, gradually lengthening the period of time that Bobo wears the collar. The idea is to get him to look forward to the presence of the head collar.

After a day or two of desensitizing Bobo to the head collar, it is time to clip your 6-foot walking lead to the metal ring that hangs below Bobo's chin. Once you do so, the additional tension he feels will cause him to object again. If he attempts to paw the head collar off, distract him by asking him to sit and quickly rewarding him with a treat. Then, quickly walk him around the room. At this point, he may try a number of techniques to free himself of the head collar, including wrapping his front legs around the lead or rearing up like a bucking bronco. You will have to take a rather stoic attitude with Bobo at this point and simply require him to walk with you. If he begins to dart out ahead, simply stop his forward motion with a few gentle pulls on the lead. Do not use too much force, because this might strain his neck. If Bobo is a small dog, hardly any pressure will be needed to stop him from pulling. You will find it remarkably easy to stop even the largest dog from charging and pulling. A few gentle pulls while saying "no, don't pull" is all it takes.

This initial attempt to walk Bobo around the room with the head collar may be difficult, but he will soon accept the situation as long as you remain committed and stick with it. What you must attempt to do during the walk is to keep your lead as loose as possible unless Bobo is pulling out ahead, at which point several light pulls from you will easily stop him. As you walk around the room, make lots of quick left and right turns and abrupt directional changes. Bobo will begin to realize that where you go, *he must now follow.* He is no longer in charge of the direction or speed of the walk. Attempt to keep him right next to you on your left side, his front legs even with your legs. If he forges out ahead, just give a gentle pull and say "no, don't pull." After walking Bobo around for a few minutes, ask him to sit, give him a treat and praise, and then remove the head collar. Practice this twice each day for several days or until Bobo begins to accept the head collar and the concept of walking without pulling.

Once Bobo is walking nicely in the home, it is time to go outside. If Bobo has successfully pawed the head collar off his muzzle in the past (some dogs are able to do this), it might be a good idea to have a second lead clipped on to Bobo's regular collar. You should hold this lead along with the one clipped to the head collar. This will prevent him from getting away from you in the event he paws off the head collar. If Bobo has no problem wearing the head collar, however, and doesn't try to get it off, using the second lead is unnecessary.

Choose a quiet area first, perhaps a yard or a residential street in the evening, when there is little going on. There should not be lots of cars or pedestrian traffic or any other dogs present. With your lead clipped to the head collar, walk Bobo around the inside of the home for a few minutes, then take him outside. Duplicate the same techniques used indoors; if he pulls, simply stop his forward motion with a gentle pull on the lead. When he is by your side on a loose lead, praise him.

Realize that when he is outside, Bobo will be much more likely to pull out and try to lead you around, just like he has always done in the past. There will be more distractions out there as well, including smells, birds, sounds, and the like, so be prepared for some antics on his part. He may show some initial frustration at not being in charge of the walk. You must remain stoic and committed through this period of behavior modification and learn to deal with his objections. They will pass, and once you get the hang of the technique, you will be amazed at how effective the head collar is at preventing Bobo from pulling you all over the place.

Once Bobo is walking nicely for you in a quiet, secluded area, it is time to take him for a real walk around your neighborhood. Be aware that Bobo will now be encountering lots of distractions, and if he has been extremely controlling and dominant, he may feel the need to stick his big nose into everything. Don't let him. It is your walk, and he is just along for the ride. Keep the pace up and the initial distance short. Take some treats along with you; randomly ask him to sit, and then reward him. This will help focus him on what you are doing. Slowly increase the duration of the walks. Remember to keep a loose lead. Also remember that Bobo's proper position is by your side, with his front legs even with your legs. Use the head collar exclusively on walks for 4 to 6 weeks.

Once Bobo has been walking nicely for you around the neighborhood for about a month or so, take him out for a walk with one lead clipped to the head collar and a second to his regular collar, as insurance. Halfway through the walk, have him sit, and reward him with praise and a treat. Then, clip your lead *off the head collar, and walk him with the lead connected to the regular collar.* Continue the walk and see what happens. If you have used the head collar properly, Bobo should not be pulling at all, even though the lead is clipped to the regular collar. You will have broken him of the habit. After a few minutes or if he starts pulling again, clip back to the head collar and take him home. Over a period of a few weeks, see if you can wean Bobo off the head collar and back onto a regular collar. Some dogs have no problem doing this. Others, particularly those who have been extremely dominant and pushy for a long time, may never be able to go for walks without the head collar. That's okay; it can remain a device that allows you to control your dog properly, the way one would a horse.

Several manufacturers also market a device known as a "no-pull harness." This harness looks much like a standard walking harness with one addition: It has two straps that connect to the collar, loop down under the dog's legs, and join up at the top of the harness at the dog's shoulders. The walking lead clips to the joining ring of these two straps, and when any pressure is put on them (either from you or the dog), the resulting tension the dog feels in its "armpit" area seems to stop the pulling.

The advantage of this system over the head collar is that there is no initial period of desensitization needed; you can just put it on Bobo and go. For dogs that simply will not tolerate wearing a head collar, this piece of equipment may be a good alternative. If Bobo is dog-aggressive, the no-pull harness will not allow you to stop him from attacking the other dog. The head collar, because it gives you control over Bobo's head, should allow you to stop the intended assault. If Bobo simply won't accept the presence of the head collar on his face, try the no-pull harness.

Solution: Teach Bobo That You Go First Through Doors

Bobo must understand that, as leader, you have the right and responsibility to go through doors first and that he must always wait his turn. As you know by now, leaders always go first, ahead of their perceived subordinates. If Bobo is a dominant, pushy dog, he will no doubt think he has the right to blow through a door ahead of you the moment it opens. He will have no desire to wait for you or anyone else to go through first. An open door is actually a good litmus test for Bobo; if he immediately goes through despite your admonitions, you most likely have a leadership problem going on between you.

Why should you teach Bobo to wait at doors? First, it is an issue of respect. He simply *must* allow you, the leader, to go through first. Pushing by you and charging out is a serious breach of leadership protocol and must be dealt with. Second, it is a sign that Bobo isn't thinking but, instead, simply reacting. "Oh, the door's open; I gotta go out there," is probably all that is going on in his head at that moment. Teaching him to wait a second or two before going through will help focus him and jog his brain into gear. Remember, one of your goals should be to get Bobo to think on his feet. A third reason to make him wait at doors is the all-important issue of safety. We have known of a number of dogs who, after charging out the front door, were struck and killed by a car or truck. Remember that Bobo has the reasoning capacity of a 2-year-old child. Would you let your 2-year-old run out the door ahead of you? Neither of them can conceive of the dangers awaiting them. It is your job as leader to protect Bobo from danger.

Also consider the safety and well-being of others. If Bobo is at all aggressive toward people, the last thing you want is to let him charge through the front door and scare the pants off your mail carrier, a jogger, or a pedestrian. If a biting incident occurred, serious liability concerns would arise, perhaps leading to your loss of insurance coverage or even the demise of Bobo. Even if he isn't aggressive, he still doesn't have the right to jump all over someone out there, especially a child, elderly person, or someone who is afraid of dogs. Bobo might also be tempted to rush out the front or back door to chase after another dog. If that dog is bigger and stronger, Bobo could be killed. His pushy, overly territorial nature could be abruptly and horrifically ended by a pushier, meaner Rottweiler or Mastiff.

We teach two methods for getting Bobo to wait at the door until after you have stepped out. The first one relies on the use of the head collar device, described in the previous section on how to get Bobo to walk on a loose lead without pulling. The second method can be used by those who do not choose to acclimate their dogs to a head collar and by those who have tried but failed to get their dogs to accept wearing one.

METHOD I

First, follow the steps in the previous section for acclimating Bobo to the head collar device. He should be at the point at which he does not object to wearing it and should be able to walk on a loose lead without pulling. With some dogs you can use his collar and have good results. Choose an archway in your home, perhaps one that leads from a hallway into the living room or kitchen. If there is a door, it should be wide open. Put a line of masking tape down on the floor where the hall and adjoining room meet. This will serve as a clear visual indication to Bobo that "here is the line you must not cross without my permission."

Clip Bobo's 6-foot walking lead onto the head collar, and slowly lead him up to the archway. When you are about 2 to 3 feet away from the tape, tell Bobo to "wait."

While watching Bobo, you step over the tape. Don't turn your back on Bobo; keep your eye on him. Ideally, you want him to wait on *his side* of the tape until you decide to allow him to proceed. If he tries to cross over with you, simply pull the lead lightly a few times back in the direction of the hallway while saying "no, wait." This should stop his forward motion and keep him on his side of the tape. Try not to step back where Bobo is. You don't want him to learn that he can manipulate *your* movements and get you back onto his side. Timing is crucial here. You must administer the pull on the lead just as Bobo *begins* to cross over, not during or after. Remember not to pull the lead too hard; the head collar will stop Bobo's forward motion very easily. Once Bobo is waiting on *his* side with you on *your* side, praise him for a "good wait." Don't use physical praise or treats at this point, as these would tend to draw Bobo over the tape to you. Just use verbal praise.

After about 10 seconds (count them off to yourself), say "okay," and walk Bobo through the archway. Praise him this time with a pat on the head, and then turn around and work the exercise again, going in the opposite direction. Work this wait exercise at the archway six to eight times a day for 2 days, with no distractions, before moving on.

On the third day, try working the wait command going out and in the front door of the home, at a time of day when there is little going on. Choose a time that does not coincide with Bobo's regular walking time so that he won't be revved up to get outside and unable to concentrate properly. Of course, once he learns the wait here at the front door, you *will* use it when taking him out for his walk or *whenever* leaving the home.

Have the front door wide open at first, with the screen door open as well, if there is one. Bring Bobo, on lead and head collar, up to the front door and tell him to wait, using the hand signal as well. Bobo will very likely want to charge through this door as he is so used to doing. You must be prepared to stop him with your lead and the head collar. This will be a learning experience for both of you. You are practicing behavior modification on a surprised Bobo. With Bobo waiting, you now step out the door, watching Bobo the whole time. If at any time he makes an effort to step through with you, pull the lead back while saying "no, wait." If he manages to get through despite your efforts, you should take him back into the house and try it again, this time attempting to be a bit quicker with the pull on the lead. Interpose your body, if necessary, to stop Bobo from going through. Once you have him waiting at the door, pause about 10 seconds and then give the "okay" command, which simply means "you can go ahead now." Walk Bobo out a few feet, then turn around and work the wait going back into the home.

Repeat this entire process five or six times, then quit and reward Bobo with a treat. Practice the wait at the front door several times a day for the next few weeks or whenever you have to take Bobo outside for a walk. Also, start working the wait with the door *closed*. This will be harder for you: In addition to controlling Bobo, you will have to open the door. When working the wait at a door that is closed, have Bobo wait a bit farther away from the door to allow for its opening. Hold the lead in your left hand and open the door with your right. At *no* time during the exercise should you allow Bobo to get between you and the door. Remember, *you go first!* After a few days of working the wait, Bobo should be getting the hang of it. Make sure you always work it at the front and back doors, going in or out. You can even continue working it at doors inside the home, but this is not as essential as working it at entrances and exits to the home.

METHOD 2

Use the following method if you cannot or will not use the head collar device:

1. Clip Bobo's 6-foot lead onto his regular collar. Bring him to the closed front door and have him sit for you in a position that will not block the opening of the door. If he sits, give him a treat and praise him. Then tell him to wait.

2. Next, open the front door a few inches while praising Bobo for a "good wait." If he tries to squeeze through, tell him *no* and close the door and walk him away. Then bring him back to the

door and repeat the process. Your goal at this point is to be able to open the door a few inches without Bobo's trying to squeeze through. Be patient; you may have to repeat this step five or six times before he gets it.

3. Once you can open the door a few inches without Bobo's charging through, you can begin opening it more and more each time. Every moment that Bobo does not try to get out the door is a victory for you. Just make sure to praise him for a good wait while he is doing so. Your goal is to be able to have the front door completely open without Bobo trying to sneak out. If he tries to, tell him *no*, then quickly close the door, walk him away, and begin the process again. Get him to understand that every time he tries to go out on his own, he gets the door shut in his face; each time he waits, he gets praised.

4. Once you are able to get Bobo to wait at a wide-open door, it is time to step through yourself. If at any time he tries to go along with you, tell him "no, wait." Have him continue to wait for 10 seconds. If Bobo succeeds in charging by you, say *no*, then take him back inside and repeat the step. Once you have successfully taught him to wait while you are outside, tell Bobo "okay" and walk him through the door. Once outside, have him sit, and reward him with a treat. Then, have him perform the wait going back into the home. If at any time he tries to bolt in, tell him *no*, shut the door, and walk him away. Your goal is to get Bobo to wait at the door, going in or out, until you give the "okay." Practice this each time you take Bobo out.

5. Work the wait command at every entrance and exit to the home. After 6 to 8 weeks, you will find that the lead may no longer be necessary. The wait will eventually become automatic to Bobo. You needn't practice it only at doorways. Try teaching Bobo to wait at curbsides or even in the middle of a field.

In addition to working the wait command at the doors of the home, you should require Bobo to wait while going in and out of cars. Many dogs have been run over while rushing out of the car the moment the owner opens the door. Working the wait, especially coming out of the car, may save Bobo's life one day. The rules are the same; you may need a helper, however, to aid you in working the wait coming out of the car. Remember that whichever method you use to teach it, the wait command builds respect, an essential ingredient of leadership. All members of the family should work the wait exercise to build universal respect. There is nothing worse than having your dog run out the door into the oncoming path of a car or truck.

Solution: Teach Bobo to Come When Called

In Chapter 3 we discussed good games and bad games and advised against playing any chase games with Bobo, particularly *you chasing him*. Leaders, you will recall, do not chase subordinates. The reverse is almost always true. Not only will a subordinate chase after its superior, it also will come whenever called. If the Alpha wolf called to the rest of his pack for help in defending a fresh kill against an invading pack and none of them came to his aid, the pack would suffer greatly. It is essential then, not only from a leadership stance but also in terms of survival, that a subordinate come when called. The Alpha would be degraded if called on to chase after recalcitrant pack members.

The same goes for you and Bobo. Most owners are not able to teach their dogs to come reliably when called, because their dogs do not clearly recognize them as true leaders. A dog that perceives itself an equal to its owner will ignore its owner's pleas to "come" if it feels it has better things to do. Why should Bobo come? What right do you, his equal, have in ordering him around? "Sorry, but I'm chasing after a poodle right now. I'll be with you later." A lack of leadership will almost always ensure that Bobo will blow you off when you call him, forcing you to chase after him, which in turn lowers your status even more. The chasing will become a game to Bobo, and guess what? He's got four legs to your two; you won't catch him until he *wants* to be caught.

Another reason that you might not be able to get Bobo to come when called could be the perception on his part that punishment is right around the corner. Many owners make the mistake of calling their dogs over to them and then punishing them for some past transgression. They often let their pups have free run of the home, inviting the inevitable house-training accident somewhere in a secluded area, perhaps in a closet or under a bed. The owner finds the mess (perhaps hours after the fact), gets angry, and immediately calls little Bobo over. "What did you do?" is usually the first thing the pup hears; he then gets his little face shoved into the mess while the foolish owner admonishes him. This pup did not learn how to avoid accidents in the home. By the time his owner found the mess, the pup had forgotten what he'd done. All he learned from his owner this time was "whenever I hear 'Come here, Bobo,' I'm going to get yelled at and then have my face shoved in feces." There is no better way to teach a dog *not to come* than this method. (Additionally, it teaches a dog to be secretive about where it eliminates, because it thinks that if you see its stool or urine, you are going to lose your cool.)

Getting Bobo to come to you is important not only in terms of leadership, but also for safety's sake. If you are walking Bobo in a busy area and your lead breaks, is he going to stay with you or run off? He may ignore your pleas to come and instead run into the street and get flattened. Or you could be running him off-lead in a park, when he takes off in pursuit of another dog or perhaps a squirrel or rabbit. Either way, if you haven't taught Bobo a rock-solid "come," he could get lost, hurt, or killed. He might even hurt someone or something else. Any way you look at it, the fault would be yours because you failed as a leader.

The two rules you must follow when teaching Bobo to come to you are as follows:

1. *Never, ever* call him to you and then punish him in any way or do anything to him that he interprets as unpleasant. This is the quickest way to teach him not to come.
2. Don't set yourself up to fail. During the learning process, Bobo should never have the option of *not coming* when you call him. For instance, if he hasn't yet learned a good off-leash "come,"

you shouldn't try to call him to you when he is romping in a field with three other dogs. He won't come, and he will learn that he can ignore you and not suffer the consequences. He will learn that he doesn't have to come and that there is nothing you can do about it. You can't catch him, so you fail as a leader. This is why most of the come exercise in this book is taught on progressively longer and longer leads; you can always *make* Bobo come to you. He will have no choice.

If you abide by the following instructions, you should be able to obtain a reliable off-leash come within 6 to 8 weeks. The technique described can be used on pups or adults; it is best, of course, to start Bobo out as young as possible. Those of you who have taught Bobo to dread the word *come* may need to change the word to something else, perhaps *here* or *front*.

Choose a quiet time of day when no other people or dogs are present. While in the home, clip Bobo's 6-foot walking lead onto his regular collar, have him sit, and give him a treat. Then, as quickly as you can, back away from him while enthusiastically saying, "Bobo, come here!" Be as animated and excited as possible. He should happily follow after you. After rapidly backing up about 6 to 8 feet, stop, crouch down, and praise him highly, perhaps giving him a treat. Work this several times the first day.

While you are still in the home, with no distractions, clip on Bobo's 8- to 10-foot lead. Holding the end of it, let Bobo do his own thing for a few minutes. Then, when he is not paying attention to you, quickly crouch down about 10 feet away and say, "Bobo, come here," with as much enthusiasm as you can muster. If he immediately comes right to you, praise him lavishly and give him a treat. If he does not come to you, tell him again to "come here" while putting some momentary tension on the lead. Most dogs will come at this point. It is very important to begin praising Bobo *the moment he begins coming over*. Do not wait until he has come all the way over before praising. He must understand that *the act of deciding to come* to you is a very desirable thing. If Bobo simply refuses to come, you can literally pull him over to you with the lead. After doing this, praise him for coming. In this way, *he has no option but to come*. The lead ensures that. Practice this indoor, on-lead come several times each day for 1 week before moving on. Don't move on until he comes every time without any tension on the leash. Include praise with anything that motivates him.

Continue to work the preceding step, only begin slowly to add distractions, one at a time, each day. A distraction can be a toy or treat placed on the floor, a television turned on, a friend sitting in a chair, or even someone outside mowing the lawn. Work this several times each day for 1 week; by the end of the week, you should be able to get Bobo to come to you, on lead, despite the distractions you have provided. Remember, he really has no choice at this stage; you can *make* him come to you, by reeling him in if necessary. Once he does begin coming to you, though, you should loosen all tension from the lead. Also, make sure not to raise your voice in anger at any time.

The next step is to work the come in a hallway in the home, with Bobo's 6-foot walking lead clipped on, but without you holding it. Have him sit at the end of a hallway, praise him, and then throw a few dog cookies down on the floor in front of him. While he is eating them, quietly back away down the hall about 8 to 10 feet. As soon as he is finished with the last cookie, crouch down and happily call him over to you. If he does come, praise and reward him. If he doesn't, try reducing the distance and calling him again. If he still won't come, walk over, pick up the end of lead, and quickly back away while saying, "Bobo, come here." Then, work the entire process over from the beginning. The hallway is used at this juncture because it denies Bobo the ability to move laterally; he can move only toward or away from you, making it fairly easy for you to grab hold of the lead if he disobeys.

Work this step of the come several times each day for 1 week or until Bobo is reliably coming to you in the hall without the need for you to grab the lead. Remember to be generous with treats at this point.

Continue working on the hallway come, only begin introducing distractions as you did in the previous step. If Bobo gets distracted and stops halfway down the hallway, firmly repeat the command "come here." If he is being difficult, continue the exercise with the 8- to 10-foot lead clipped on. If he stops to play with something, simply say "come here" again while putting momentary tension on the lead. If he still ignores you, simply reel him in. Remember that if you are having difficulties, it is perfectly okay to back up a step or two. Don't move on until each step has been perfected.

Once you have Bobo coming to you down the hallway with just his 6-foot lead clipped on him, you should begin turning a corner and calling him from there, out of his immediate sight. Clip his 6-foot lead on, and walk away. Go around the corner, then crouch down and call him with great enthusiasm. If you have gone through the previous five steps, Bobo should happily come right to you. When he does, give him a great treat and praise him lavishly. If he doesn't, repeat the command "come here." If he still won't come, walk over and grab his lead, quickly lead him to where you had been, and praise him for a "good come here." Continue working this step until you can get Bobo to come to you reliably from any part of the home. Do not move on until this has been accomplished.

Take Bobo out into a fenced, secluded yard, with his 8- to 10-foot lead clipped on. Holding the end of the lead, let Bobo get distracted while you quietly get as far away as the lead will allow. With the lead loose, crouch down and happily call him to you. If he comes, praise and reward him with a great treat. If he doesn't (and he might not; being outside is a great distraction to most dogs), repeat the command "come here," and put some momentary tension on the lead. If he still doesn't come, you can reel him in to you. When he is finally back to you, praise him, even if you had to reel him in. Work this step twice each day until Bobo immediately and reliably comes to you outside, on the 8- to 10-foot lead.

Purchase a 20- to 30-foot lead at the pet store (or make one yourself out of clothesline), or invest in a retractable lead, also available at the pet store. Retractable leads are spring-loaded and can change length from zero to 30 feet at the touch of a button. Clip whichever lead you have purchased onto Bobo's collar. Take him out into the yard and let him get distracted. Attempt to get at least 20 feet away from him, then crouch down and call him with as much enthusiasm as possible. If he comes, praise and reward him. If he doesn't, say "come here" again while putting momentary tension on the lead. If he still doesn't come, reel him in. By this point, Bobo should be conditioned to realize that *he has no option* but to come. Work the come on this long lead until Bobo is coming reliably every time.

Continue to work the come with the long lead, but begin introducing distractions, such as toys on the grass or two friends playing Frisbee. You must get Bobo to understand that he must come to you every time, no matter what is going on. Don't move on until this step has been perfected.

Take Bobo out into the same secluded, fenced yard on his 6-foot walking lead. Make sure there are no distractions. Have him sit, drop the leash, and step back 6 to 10 feet. Then, crouch down and happily call him to you. If he comes, praise him and give him an extra-special treat, perhaps a slice of hot dog or piece of chicken. Continue working this step; *gradually* increase your distance from Bobo until you can get him to come to you from 20 to 30 feet away. At this point, Bobo does have the option of not coming; however, by this time he should be sufficiently conditioned to know that coming is a great thing that gets rewarded. If at any point Bobo shows signs of not coming, go back to using the long lead. Then work back up to this step again. Take your time, and limit distractions until Bobo performs perfectly. *Do not at any time chase after Bobo* if he refuses to come. Instead, walk away from him, and sit down. He should eventually wander over, whereupon you can praise him and clip on your lead.

Continue the preceding step, only begin introducing distractions. Remember to back up a step if Bobo becomes difficult. Then, take Bobo to a fairly busy park, and work the come with the long lead. Remember always to reward him with a great treat when he does come. If he gets distracted, you can insist that he come to you by reeling him in. Work this several times each week for a few weeks.

If you have worked the previous steps consistently over a period of 6 to 8 weeks, you should be ready to try an off-leash come in the park. If you still don't trust your dog loose in the park, don't try it. Try it at first from only 10 feet away, and gradually lengthen the distance. Reward Bobo with a great treat each time he comes. You might also bring a friend with you; have him or her walk Bobo out about 40 or 50 feet from you. Then crouch down and call Bobo, instructing your friend beforehand to release the lead when you say "come." Bobo should come to you like a rocket. When he does, give him a piece of hot dog or chicken. Then have your friend repeat the exercise. Get Bobo to "slingshot" back and forth between you and your friend, slowly lengthening the distance until a distance of 50 to 100 yards is no problem.

Following the preceding steps should provide you with a dog that is ready and willing to come to you. Make sure not to rush the training, however. Remember that any bad habit that Bobo has developed will probably take 6 to 8 weeks to truly change. Also, make sure that while you are teaching the come you do not take Bobo to the park and let him run loose. This will defeat all the training we have discussed so far. Be patient and you will prevail.

Five

LEADERS CONTROL THEIR SPACE AND POSSESSIONS

The 2-year-old male wolf walked over to the Alpha male's high spot near the old jack pine and lay down. The largest wolf in the pack, he outweighed the Alpha by at least 10 pounds and would perhaps one day be his successor. A well-chewed femur bone from an old bull moose lay there. He picked it up in his mouth and began to gnaw on it. The bone had been a favorite of the Alpha ever since the pack brought the moose down 2 days before. Now, with the Alpha male and his mate out scouting the northern perimeter of their territory, the young male felt comfortable and strong, there in his leader's spot that overlooked the entire meadow.

When the young male heard the two young pups coming down the ridge, he knew both Alphas would soon be home. He felt good about that, yet he did not think to get up or even to stop chewing on the bone he had coveted for the last few weeks.

The pups cavorted into the meadow closely followed by their mother, the Alpha female. She trotted in, circled the resting pack, then headed over to the high spot, where the young male was resting and chewing. She sniffed the scene, and gruffed at him several times as if to warn him of his foolishness. He was too enraptured with the bone to respond respectfully to her. She paced nervously and waited.

Just then she caught sight of her mate, who was quietly sitting 20 yards above them on the hill that led to the ridge trail. He was looking down on the scene with calm indifference, as if slightly disappointed and somewhat bored. The young male abruptly stopped his chewing and scented the air, the bone still hanging loosely from his mouth. As he

looked above, the Alpha female and her pups quietly left the scene and
joined the others below in`the meadow. The young male scanned the
woods above him and caught sight of his leader calmly staring at him,
still in the sitting position, unmoving. Standing now, he dropped the bone
and continued to meet the Alpha's gaze. Then the Alpha lowered his
head slightly, turning the gaze into a glare. `The young male broke eye
contact, batted the bone with his big right paw, and sauntered over to
the meadow to tease one of the juveniles into a game of chase. The
Alpha male came down the hill to his spot, lifted his leg on the old jack
pine, and lay down, his head resting on the worn femur bone of the old
bull moose.

The leader has privileges. He earns them every day by keeping
order and ensuring the survival of the pack. Once afforded these
privileges, he openly displays them as a means to reinforce further his
position in the minds of the pack members. Privileges are spoils of
high position in the pack and are taken very seriously by all members.
The Alpha male had claimed the high spot near the jack pine as his.
Its vantage point allowed him to survey the pack's meadow easily and
caused his subordinates literally to look up to him. It was his throne,
so to speak, and to have another male wolf occupy it was a serious
breach of protocol and a serious challenge to the pecking order.

The challenger did not commit a heinous act, however; to the
contrary, he simply displayed his growing status in the pack. As a
possible future leader, he needed to begin exerting and testing his
growing dominance. Intermittent challenges are almost welcomed by
the Alpha so that he can display his authority, which further
reinforces his sovereignty. Challenges also keep him on his toes and
in touch with the ever-changing pack dynamic.

That said, the young upstart hadn't the right or the courage to
usurp his leader's favorite spot. He'd displayed his growing self-
confidence while the leader was gone, but on his return was quickly
vanquished with a simple glare. A stronger challenge would have
been met by a stronger response from the leader, perhaps even
resulting in physical confrontation.

The young male wolf, in addition to usurping the Alpha's spot,
chose to commandeer the leader's favorite possession as well. The

bone was the Alpha's favorite object, and the other pack members knew and respected this. By laying claim to the leader's possession, the young male again displayed a disrespect for the authority of his superior. He had broken two of the cardinal rules: *Don't mess with the leader's space*, and *leave his possessions alone*. The Alpha handled the young upstart's insubordination in classic leader fashion: He made his displeasure with the young wolf known through intense eye contact, effectively rectifying the situation without having to resort to physical confrontation or violence.

Bobo knows the rules regarding space and possessions as well as any wolf does. So when you find him snoozing in your favorite easy chair or on your king-sized bed, it isn't because he's tired. He chooses those places because they are the most desirable in the home, and thinking himself dominant, he feels he has a right to them. In effect he is saying, "I think these spots are the best in the home, so I'm going to claim them. After all, I'm the leader, am I not?" If you acquiesce, thinking that he's tired or that you don't want to disturb him, then he has won and you have lost major leadership points. Consider also the dog that decides to lie down right in the middle of the entranceway to the living room. Most owners politely step around the resting dog, trying not to disturb him; the dog succeeds in *training its owners* to appease him (exactly what a leader does). These mistakes, added up over the years, can create a dominant mind-set in the dog, which can lead to a myriad of problems, including aggression.

Bobo is territorial by nature. The desire to claim dominion over a defined space is deeply ingrained in the canine psyche and is derived in part by the need to have unrestricted access to a productive hunting ground. Dogs are also particular about whom they let into their personal space or have physical contact with. This "zone of personal space" is a privileged area. Those allowed in either have great status or are needed for some purpose, such as grooming or mating. Two male wolves close to each other in the pecking order have much less physical contact than a mated pair, for example. When a dog is resting comfortably in a favorite area, therefore, it will allow others to approach it only if they are of higher status or are offering some desired service, such as grooming.

A story was related to us last year that serves to illustrate how a dog can attain complete control over its owners in terms of controlling space. An elderly couple went shopping at a local department store and, for a change, decided to take Ozzie with them in the car. Ozzie, a 3-year-old unneutered Harlequin Great Dane, weighed over one hundred and fifty pounds and would respond only to the wife and only if she bribed him with treats. Ozzie didn't like or listen to the husband and had on several occasions bitten him. While they were in the store, the couple heard a store page regarding a car in the parking lot with its lights on. It was theirs, and the husband went out to shut off the lights before the battery went dead. When he reached the car, Ozzie began barking and snarling at him. Try as he might, the husband couldn't get into the car without getting bitten by Ozzie, who by this time was biting at the door and steering wheel in his eagerness to guard "his" car.

After 15 minutes, the wife, concerned about her husband's whereabouts, went out to check on him. She found him staring at the car from 20 feet away, wondering what to do. She tried to get into the car, but Ozzie wouldn't even let her in. Finally, the wife went back into the store, bought a box of dog biscuits, and got access to the car through bribery. This true but absurd story illustrates just how out of hand some owners allow their dogs to become, especially with regard to controlling space.

The leader of the pack can go anywhere he or she wants to. There is no place the leader cannot go: No room, no yard, no bed, no chair he or she cannot occupy at any time, day or night. Subordinates, on the other hand, are denied access to areas claimed by the leader. To occupy these areas would be an insult to the leader's status and would call for swift discipline. If Bobo thinks that he is the dominant member of the pack, he will defend what he considers to be his territory, be it a chair, bed, corner of a room, or space beneath a table. We have had hundreds of clients come to us for help in stopping their dogs from biting them when they simply try to sit down in their easy chairs or get into their own beds at night. Their dominant, pushy dogs had laid claim to these comfy spots and, thinking themselves the leader, felt justified in disciplining their subordinate owners by growling and biting. Understand that this is not deviant behavior on the dogs' part; they are just doing what any leader would do to a misbehaving subordinate. Remember, being dominant gives you the right to discipline the pack.

In addition to coveting certain areas of the home, a dominant dog may also claim and defend whatever objects it desires, from bones or balls to the owner's socks and shoes. Again, if you have allowed Bobo to become dominant, you have given him, the "leader," the right to discipline others in the pack for trying to steal back these items, even if the item happens to be a belt that you need to wear to work that day. If Bobo is dominant, he is likely, for example, to lie under a table chewing on a bone and to growl at or bite anyone who tries to move him or take the bone away. Most biting incidents involving children take place because of this possessive/aggressive attitude: A five-year-old sees Bobo under the table with a toy or bone and decides to crawl under there and play with him. Bobo sees this as an invasion of his space and an attempt to steal his possession and quite logically decides to discipline through biting. He isn't evil or brain-damaged. He's just dominant.

As the leader of your pack, you must determine where your coveted areas are and deny Bobo access to them. The bed, for example, is your sanctuary. It is the highest place, and it should never be shared with a subordinate. Allowing Bobo to sleep with you is one of the biggest mistakes you can make, because it tells him in dog language that you consider him your equal. The same goes for your easy chair or anywhere else you consider a human resting place. As leader, you must also make clear to Bobo that everything in and around the home belongs to you and that he gets to play with certain items only when you, the leader, decide it's okay.

Goal: To Reclaim Your Territory

As leader, it is crucially important for you to be able to go anywhere you want to and to lay claim to a desired area or possession withou any interference from Bobo, who must be taught that he is merely a guest in your home.

Solution: Keep Bobo Off the Bed

Ben, a client of ours, came to us recently with a major aggression problem involving his beautiful 3-year-old male Akita, Khruschev. The client had allowed Khruschev to sleep in bed with him since the dog was 8 weeks old. Recently, Ben had asked his girlfriend, Kathy, to move in with him. Kathy loved dogs and was sure that Khruschev would quickly grow to love and accept her.

While Kathy was in the bathroom getting ready for their first night together in the home, Khruschev, as usual, climbed into bed with Ben, who automatically began stroking the dog's thick coat. Kathy then walked into the bedroom and tried to get into bed with Ben, who was cuddling Khruschev. The dog growled softly.

"Don't worry, hon, that's just his play growl," said Ben. Trusting Ben's judgment, Kathy slipped in under the covers. Khruschev bared his teeth and snarled. Kathy looked to Ben, still wanting to trust in his judgment.

"Easy boy, it's okay," Ben said, petting the dog. At that moment, Khruschev lunged out at Kathy, biting her on the arm. Although the bite did not break the skin, it was nevertheless a painful and frightening experience for Kathy.

"He must be afraid of you, Kath." At that point, Kathy lowered herself to the floor. "Maybe I should sleep next to the bed tonight, in my sleeping bag. He probably just needs to get used to my scent."

"Yeah," agreed Ben. Shaken by the experience, he continued to stroke the dog. Kathy slept on the carpeted floor next to the bed that night and for the next week, while Ben and Khruschev slept soundly in the bed. After trying and failing several more times to get into the bed with Ben, Kathy had had it and asked Ben to choose between her and the dog.

The next day he came to us for help. We were amazed at the story and couldn't believe that anyone would rationalize a dog's bad behavior to this extent. Ben had pampered and babied his dog all its life, and he was now surprised at the outcome. Khruschev was an Akita, an instinctively dominant breed that needs strong leadership from Day 1. He'd been treated instead like the heroine of "The Princess and the Pea"; nothing was good enough for him, as far as Ben was concerned. The biggest mistake Ben had made was letting the dog share his bed from puppyhood on, giving Khruschev the idea that he was on equal footing with Ben. Furthermore, Ben had never done any obedience training with the bratty dog. Kathy further compounded the problem by sleeping on the floor of the bedroom, lower than Khruschev.

First, we took Khruschev into our facility for 2 weeks of intensive behavior-modification work. He was extremely dominant and tried to bite us many times during the first few days. By the end of the 2-week period, however, he had begrudgingly accepted his new position as subordinate. We required him to learn basic obedience and to obey without question any human that asked him to do something, however trivial he thought it was. Then, we taught the obedience techniques to Ben and Kathy and insisted that Kathy work Khruschev's obedience as much as or more than Ben did, to get the dog to accept her as a leader instead of someone to bite at. We told Ben that his dog needed to be banished forever from the bed and bedroom. In fact, Khruschev was demoted to sleeping downstairs in the den. Within 3 months, relative peace had been restored to the house, and Khruschev finally knew what his new place was in the pecking order. He was made to accept the fact that Kathy, a new member of "the pack," had more status than he and therefore deserved respect. Once this was accomplished, the biting stopped.

The leader of the pack always sleeps in the highest, warmest, most comfortable place. That's the way it is. Even among pups in the litter, this instinctive behavior can be observed. The most dominant pup usually sleeps closest to the mother or is located in the center of the sleeping litter, whereas those less dominant occupy areas farther out, often closer to the perimeter of the whelping box. The more dominant a dog is in its pack, the higher up it will sleep. Height, therefore, is literally a measurement of status among dogs.

When you took Bobo home as a little pup, you may have allowed him to sleep in your bed, at least for the first few weeks. After all, he was so cute and cuddly and seemed to want to be close to you and the warmth your bed provided. Toy dogs, especially, are often allowed to share the owner's bed, sometimes for their entire lives. Right from the start, therefore, Bobo was taught that he had equal status with you. You immediately began to undermine your leadership, while at the same time boosting his. Most dominant/aggressive dogs have been allowed to sleep in bed with their owners (or the owner's children) from a very early age.

Moving Bobo out of the bed is a crucial step in gaining leadership over him. It will not be a change that he'll get used to overnight, however (no pun intended). By moving him out of your bed, you will be saying, "We are no longer on equal terms. I am now higher than you in the pack." Bobo won't give up the bed easily. He may cry, whine, bark, and attempt to sneak back up onto the bed in the middle of the night or when you are not around. You must be committed to keeping him out of your bed even if it means closing your bedroom door or using a dog crate.

In order to increase your status in Bobo's eyes, you simply must sleep higher than he does, in your bed, and relegate him to a lower position. Following are the steps to achieving this objective:

1. At bedtime, clip Bob's training lead onto his collar.
2. Place a blanket or rug on the floor next to your bed and encourage Bobo to lie down on it, perhaps giving him a treat if he complies. Then, get into your bed.
3. If he jumps up on the bed, grasp his lead (not his collar), tell him "no, off!" and physically guide him off the bed and back onto the rug or blanket.
4. If Bobo continues to jump up onto the bed, take him over to the door, tether his lead to the doorknob, and go back to bed or put him in another area of the house. Now it is physically impossible for him to jump up onto your bed. Ignore all whining or tantrums. Don't respond at all, even by yelling. Remember, Bobo will take negative attention over no attention at all.

5. An alternative to tethering Bobo to the door would be to have him sleep in a plastic travel crate next to your bed. A simple way to prevent him from jumping up, it also affords him his own little "sanctuary" and allows him to stay in the bedroom, albeit at a lower position than you, the leader.

Using the crate also requires training to get Bobo accustomed to it. This task is aided by the fact that dogs are by nature denning animals. They instinctively want to rest in a small, cozy space, which creates a feeling of security as well as preserving body warmth. Bobo is no different. From the time he is a pup, you should provide him with his own plastic travel crate and teach him to accept being in it for extended periods of time. By restricting Bobo to a crate at night, you will be helping him to learn proper house-training manners. Dogs by nature prefer not to eliminate in or near their sleeping area, partly for cleanliness, but also because this would attract predators to the den. If Bobo is loose in the home at night, he has the opportunity to wander off somewhere, eliminate, and then go back to his sleeping area. Not so if he is in a crate. He has no choice but to wait for you to let him out to eliminate. The crate therefore facilitates house-training better than any other device. It will also save your house from destruction when you leave Bobo home alone.

In addition, periodic use of the crate can have a calming influence on a puppy or adult dog and can help improve overall focus. It can also be used for "time-outs," when Bobo has done something uncalled for and needs to be temporarily isolated from the rest of the pack. A time-out is not overt punishment but simply a way of telling the dog that his stupid behavior is not pleasing to the rest of the pack.

A great way to get a pup or adult dog used to its crate is to feed it *in the crate*, with the door open or completely removed at first. Place Bobo's food dish at the center of the crate and sit next to it while he investigates. Most dogs, if at all food-motivated, will go in and begin eating. The use of treats tossed into the crate also can help teach Bobo that the crate is a good place to be. If the crate is large enough, you can even get down on the floor and stick the upper half of your body into it. This is not recommended if you are dealing with a dominant dog. Bobo will go right in to check out what on earth you are doing. When he does, give him a treat or a kiss.

After a day or two of feeding Bobo in the crate, try quietly closing the door while he is busy eating. Sit there talking to him, and leave him in there for a minute or two after he is done eating. Gradually lengthen the amount of time he spends in the crate, and begin leaving the room for longer and longer periods. If Bobo begins to whine at this point, just ignore it. Leaving a radio or television on can help ease his separation anxiety, so try this if necessary. Eventually, you should be able to leave Bobo in the crate for extended periods of time.

If Bobo is a very dominant/aggressive dog with an ongoing history of biting you or other members of the family, you may need to banish him completely from all bedrooms in the home. This type of dog needs to sleep in the lowest part of the home, perhaps in a crate in the hallway downstairs or in the basement. This is not meant as punishment but rather as a message to Bobo that he is now lowest on the totem pole. Any tantrums that he throws (and he will throw them) must be ignored; they will subside eventually, and he will begin to see that you are serious about exerting your status with regard to where both of you sleep.

Do *not* allow Bobo to sleep with your children. This bad habit teaches the dog that these little people are merely "littermates" to be dealt with on equal footing. Bobo will learn no respect for them at all and could easily decide to use aggression on them as a means of disciplining. Some very dominant dogs even attempt to mount a human child as a means of control, the way they sometimes do within the species. Mounting among canines often is not related to the sexual act but is instead a strong method of challenging another's position. If you see this behavior in Bobo, you know it is time to reevaluate seriously the relationship between child and dog.

Remember that love has nothing to do with it. A dog is always trying to determine where it fits in the pecking order of the family. If it can climb past a few children on the way to the top, it will. You must help all humans in the family, including the children, to gain leadership over Bobo.

Solution: Keep Bobo Off the Furniture

Many of our clients have dominant dogs that commandeer sofas and easy chairs in the home and bite anyone who tries to move them or sit next to them. These dogs are thinking, "How dare you try to move me from my resting place!" Pampered and placated their whole lives, these pushy dogs feel completely justified in denying their "subordinates" access to such special resting places. As leader of your pack, you should deny Bobo access to furniture anywhere in the home unless that piece of furniture is there expressly for him. By allowing him free access to your easy chair, for example, you tell him that he has equal status and can assert himself against you.

1. While Bobo is in the home, and you are there to watch him, keep his training lead clipped on him. If at any time he jumps up onto the furniture (whether you are on it or not), grasp the lead, tell him "no, off," and guide him off.
2. Once he is off, tell him "good off," then sit back down.
3. If he continues to jump up, simply bring him over to a door and tether the lead to the knob. Then ignore him for at least 10 minutes, even if he becomes obnoxious.
4. After this period, if he is quiet, go over and release him and sit down again. If he jumps up again, tether him and leave him for a longer period. If you practice this consistently for 6 to 8 weeks, Bobo will eventually learn that he can't win.
5. While you are gone, put Bobo in a crate or a room without furniture. We don't want him to think as long as you're not there the furniture belongs to him.

Some of you have dogs that you want to invite up into your lap to pet and hold. If your dog is not extremely dominant/aggressive and has gone through the previous exercise, you can begin teaching the "up" and "off" commands. Invite Bobo "up" by patting your knee and saying "Bobo, up." Praise him, then tell him "okay, Bobo, off." At that point, use his lead to guide him off you onto the floor, and then praise him by saying "good off." Repeat this on a regular basis; eventually he will begin to respond to both commands. If you are going to allow him up at all, make sure it is by invitation only and that he learns to get off when you say so. Remember to stay calm through the entire procedure.

Solution: Keep Bobo Out from Under Tables and Chairs and Out of Corners

In addition to going up onto furniture, dominant dogs often lay claim to areas underneath dinner or coffee tables, or corners of the room. An owner who does not have proper leadership often gets bitten while trying to extricate Bobo from under the dinner table so that family and guests can eat in peace. The opportunity for Bobo to do this must be eliminated. He must not be given the chance to take over and defend any area in your territory, no matter how small.

1. Clip on Bobo's training lead, and leave it on while he is in the home with you.
2. If Bobo goes under a piece of furniture or in a far corner, pick up the end of the lead and physically move him out to a place that is more acceptable to you, preferably in the middle of the room. Make sure that the lead you use is at least 8 feet long so that you are able to grab the end of it without risking getting bitten. If you can't reach the end of the lead, use something, besides your hand, to reach in and slide the lead to where you can reach it safely. If he returns to the undesired area, move him again and tether the lead to a doorknob to prevent any further transgressions.
3. Leave Bobo tethered for at least half an hour, and during that time, ignore him completely.
4. After the allotted time, untether Bobo from the doorknob, but leave the lead clipped onto his collar. Each time he tries to lay claim to a secluded area, repeat the process. Be consistent. After 6 to 8 weeks, Bobo will get the message. Remember that dogs learn through repetition over a long period of time.

One of the trainers at our facility adopted a 7-month-old Rottweiler mix off the street, from a rural wooded section of northern California. He'd found out through some investigation that the dog had been living a feral life with a pack of strays; they survived any way they could, eating roadkill and garbage and hunting rats, squirrels, and other small game. This dog had been at the bottom of his pack and had to fight just to hold onto the smallest morsel. When the trainer took him home, the dog thought he had died and gone to heaven. Everything was provided for, and nothing had to be fought over. Old habits die hard, though, and this dog did not know any other way to be. When given a chew toy, therefore, it would guard it zealously, snapping at anyone who came near.

We had to brainstorm on this for a while before coming up with a solution. First, we developed a common language and gained some control through obedience training. Then, we developed a plan that involved overloading the dog's environment with chew toys. We provided him with so many that no *one* toy became invaluable to him. This was an unusual case. The dog's possessive nature was caused not by dominance but rather by fear of starvation, learned from infancy. Normally we would have *restricted* access to toys while simultaneously training in obedience. Had we used this method (normally used for possessive/aggressive dogs), he would not have responded well and, in fact, probably would have gotten worse. This is an example of being in touch with the dog and getting to the root cause of a problem behavior. The dog responded well and now lives happily with the owner.

If Bobo is showing any possessive aggression over toys, chews, or even items such as shoes or socks, chances are it is because he thinks he has a right to them, being (in his mind) the leader. Again, here is an example of a specific behavior problem having as its root cause the lack of leadership skills on the part of the owner. The leader of the pack (you) has dominion over the territory that the pack occupies. Any objects that exist in this area belong to the leader. Owners may allow the others in the pack to use or play with these items if they are so inclined. At any time, however, if they choose, they can reclaim the items without argument.

In your home, Bobo is simply a guest. He does not own anything. He does not pay rent or utilities. He lives there by your grace. Nothing in the home, not his bowl, his toys, his rug, his collar, or even his food, belongs to him. All of it is yours, period. If he has been unintentionally taught by you and your family to be leader, however, he will assume that everything belongs to him, including your shoes, car, toothbrush, down jacket, eyeglasses, and children. If Bobo decides to grab your left penny loafer, for instance, crawl under the table and chew it to bits, it is his right as leader to do so, and if you (a subordinate) try to stop him, he is totally within his rights to bite you as discipline for being out of line and for not respecting his leadership. That is the cross you bear when you mistakenly teach Bobo that he is the leader. He thinks he has the right and responsibility to discipline (bite) his pack if any of them are insubordinate, because that behavior threatens the solidarity of the pack.

Solution: Teach Bobo That Everything in the Home is Yours

You must teach your dog that everything in the house belongs to you and that gaining access to any objects, including dog toys, must come only through the permission of you, the leader.

The first step in teaching Bobo that you have dominion over possessions is to regain control over them. To this end, pick up all items from the floor of your home, including not only his toys but your things as well. Shoes, belts, clothing, and the like should all be removed along with his toys to prevent Bobo from getting the opportunity to grab something of his own volition and guard it. From now on, availability is under your control. He has to look to you for any object of desire.

Many dogs first get into the habit of commandeering their owner's personal items because the items are inundated with the owner's scent, which most dogs (especially pups) like to have around. Your scent is familiar and reassuring to Bobo, so he naturally wants to savor anything that contains it. The remote control for your television or VCR, for instance, is a favorite for many dogs because it is quite possibly the most handled item in the home. Your scent permeates it, and Bobo is attracted to it. The same goes for socks, underwear, and shoes. You have also showed him that these items are important to you, so they must be valuable. None of these or any other personal items should be left out for Bobo to play with or covet. If you do leave your belongings lying around, you are simply setting Bobo up to fail. This isn't the sign of a good leader, so pick thing up and put them away. If you don't, he'll either destroy them or claim them as his own, possibly precipitating an aggressive confrontation with you.

Do not leave Bobo's toys or chews out on the floor either if he is at all possessive of them. If you do, he will slowly begin to think that they belong to him and that you had nothing to do with providing them. In his mind, if the toys and chews are always available on the floor, they aren't coming from you, but rather from the floor. He is finding them himself and therefore feels as if he is responsible for bringing them into his life. He will not connect the items with you at all and may in fact (especially if he is very dominant) try to deny you access to them by growling or snapping at you. For the time being, therefore, you should pick up all toys and chews and store them in a drawer when you aren't present.

After you have picked up all items, choose a random time of day to clip Bobo's lead on (if it isn't already on him), and bring out a few of his toys and chews. Make Bobo earn the right to have them by doing something for you, the leader. It can be something as simple as a sit or perhaps performing a trick he knows such as shake or roll over. The idea is to get him to recognize that he has to satisfy some condition that you have set before he gets a reward, in this case a toy or a chew. Let him play with an item for a few minutes, then pick up the lead and ask him to sit (if he doesn't know how, a "come here, Bobo" will suffice). Praise him, and offer him a treat. When you do this, he will probably drop the item. You should pick it up and praise him for a "good give." (Do not grab hold of the toy if Bobo has been extremely aggressive in the past and has bitten you. Instead, make him sit, then offer a cookie to get the toy away.) It helps if the item is big enough that you can grasp firmly without having to put your ha directly into Bobo's mouth. Do not play tug of war! If he does not release the item, take and attach his lead and walk him over to where he can't get under anything, and ignore him. If the item is not important to you it won't be as important to him.

Don't let Bobo get into the habit of taking a toy, chew, or something of yours and going under a table with it. He may begin guarding the item from you or other family members, growling and snapping at anyone who tries to retrieve it. If he does this, do not try to grab him by the collar. Instead, pick up the end of the lead (which you should keep on him while he is in the home and supervised), and make him leave the inaccessible area. Then ask him to sit, and try the treat method mentioned previously as a method to retrieve the item. If at all possible, avoid conflict. Attempt instead to get Bobo to think that good things will happen if he surrenders the item.

After a play session with the toys or chews, collect the items and put them away. In this way, you will slowly recondition Bobo to realize that you are the source of the play items and that you dictate where and when he will get to play with them. This fact will raise your leadership status enormously in his eyes.

Solution: Avoid Possessive Behavior by Teaching Bobo the "Leave It" Command

Sometimes you will not be able to avoid having items around that Bobo finds appealing. Guests may come over with their small child, for instance, and bring with them the child's toys, which can end up strewn all over the living room carpet. In situations like this, it is convenient to be able to tell Bobo to leave something alone, even if it happens to be lying right in his path. "Leave it" simply means that whatever is there on the floor, counter, or table, Bobo must pay it no mind, no matter if it is a toy, slipper, or pork chop. *Leave it* means leave it be, completely, until I tell you otherwise. Teaching Bobo that certain items are off-limits to him is an excellent way of lowering his inflated status in the pecking order, while at the same time raising ours. Remember that there is nothing cruel about denying Bobo privileges afforded to you or other humans. To the contrary, canine psychology demands it.

1. Clip on Bobo's lead, if it is not already on.
2. Place a few items on the living room floor that Bobo will be interested in. Include a toy, a treat, and something of yours, perhaps a sock or shirt.
3. Starting with him sitting on your left side, begin slowly walking Bobo around the room. Make sure you are holding the lead about 2 or 3 feet from the collar, and try to keep it as loose as possible.
4. When Bobo is approximately 2 to 3 feet away from the first item, tell him in a commanding voice, "Bobo, leave it." He will of course ignore the command because he hasn't yet learned it. As soon as you see that his intention is to go for the item, say "leave it" and quickly lead him away in the other direction. After you do this, have him sit, and reward him with a treat. Anticipating the moment that he goes for the item is important. Turning him away from the item must occur just as he commits to going for it and before he actually gets to it. Use of the head collar works well for this, as you can easily turn his head away from the forbidden item.
5. Continue walking Bobo past items on the floor, giving him the "leave it" command before he gets to them. Use your lead to turn him away before he picks an item up in his mouth, then have him sit and reward him with a treat. Eventually, he will see that the sooner he ignores the item on the floor, the sooner he will get rewarded.
6. Bobo will soon begin to ignore the items when you command him to. The first time this occurs, praise him greatly, perhaps giving him a treat and a pat on the head.
7. Practice the "leave it" command at least once each day for several weeks. Keep adding new temptations and practice in different locations. Eventually, Bobo will learn to leave something alone when you ask him to, without the need for the lead. Soon only a pet on the head will be sufficient praise; you needn't continue using treats.

When he has learned this response well enough, Bobo should leave alone food that you drop on the floor near him or even the family cat. We know of several instances in which this command saved dogs who were about to nose up to other, much more aggressive dogs. One of our own dogs promptly responded to a "leave it" command when he began to investigate innocently a diamondback rattlesnake that had slithered across a hiking trail in the hills of southern California.

Solution: Teach Bobo to Move Out of Your Way

Leaders do not accommodate subordinates. If a dominant dog is walking down a hallway and a subordinate dog is lying in the way, the subordinate dog should get up and move to let the dominant dog pass by. Most owners, however, step over or move around Bobo if he is in the way to avoid disturbing him. It is the polite thing to do, but it isn't the correct thing to do, from a leadership standpoint. When you appease Bobo by moving out of his way, you are telling him that you recognize his right to control and monopolize that spot as well as implying that you do not have the right to disturb him. A loss of status in his eyes is inevitable.

1. Make sure Bobo's lead is clipped onto his collar.
2. If Bobo is lying in the middle of a hallway that you wish to walk down and he shows no signs of moving as you approach, simply pick up the end of the lead, say "move" or "get," and move him aside with the lead. Once he is out of your way, praise him by saying "good move" or "good get."

If you repeat this procedure whenever Bobo is in the way and refuses to move, he soon will move for all members of your family without the need for the lead (provided everyone is involved in the training). He also should learn to stop placing himself in the middle of a well-traveled area or at least quickly move out of the way when someone is coming.

Continue working this procedure whenever necessary. Within 6 to 8 weeks, it will become routine to Bobo, and the problem should disappear. He should understand that, as leader, you have the right to walk wherever you desire in your territory without interruption.

Marking is one of the primary ways that a dog claims territory and expresses dominance over others. When a dog marks an area or item with a spray of urine, it leaves its scent there as a marker for other dogs. Marking is a statement of ownership or control of an area. If two dogs are together in a yard, for instance, and the subordinate dog lifts his leg and urinates on a tree, the dominant dog will almost certainly go over to that tree and mark over his friend's statement. The subordinate dog at this point will most likely refrain from marking the spot again, out of respect. This is interpreted by the dominant dog as a definite statement of submission. His status then rises appropriately. Defecation is used in much the same way as urination, leaving a strong message that says "this is my place."

When you take Bobo for a walk, chances are that he decides when and where to urinate or defecate. You, of course, cannot mark over his leavings without getting arrested. This sets up a dilemma: Bobo is marking the places of his choice, and you, the leader, are acquiescing, blatantly telling him that you accept his dominance without question. How then, without actually marking yourself, can you prevent Bobo from thinking that you are accepting his dominance?

Solution: Control Where and When Bobo Relieves Himself

When you take Bobo out for a walk, think in terms of it being *your* walk, not his, and that he is just along for the ride. As leader, that should be your attitude, and he should accept that. You are not there to serve his needs; rather, he is there to keep you company. When you take Bobo out for a walk, therefore, do exactly that: Walk. Don't stop every 10 feet to let him sniff or urinate or defecate. Just leave the house, allow him a few moments to eliminate in a favorite spot close by, and start walking at a comfortable pace, expecting him to keep up. If he stubbornly tries to hold you up by investigating something or pulling you off to the side, tell him "no, let's go," and keep walking briskly. Do not let him bully you or decide when to stop on his own.

When you decide that it is time to stop, do so, and then say "okay Bobo, hurry up," or "okay, go potty," or whatever you decide on. Give him a minute or two, and if he doesn't relieve himself, say "okay, let's go," and begin walking again, briskly, even if he tries to lag. The goal is to teach Bobo that you are taking over the timing and location of his elimination. By determining this function, you prevent his interpreting your lack of marking behavior as a sign of submission to him.

If you use this procedure on all walks, you will discover that Bobo eventually will begin to eliminate *on command.* This result can be extremely convenient, especially when you want to get him to do his thing for you quickly, perhaps right before bedtime or when it is cold or rainy. There is nothing worse than having to walk your dog up and down the street endlessly in bad weather, waiting for him to choose a spot. This method will prevent that from happening if you stick to it long enough.

If Bobo eliminates in a yard, you can still invoke this principle by getting him to go in a specific place instead of anywhere he wants. Take Bobo out (on lead) to a desirable spot in the yard, perhaps a 5-by 10-foot area, and encourage him to go by saying "hurry up" or "go potty," or whatever you choose. Give him a few minutes. If he doesn't go, bring him back in the house and try it again in half an hour. Eventually, he will go where you want him to, and when he does, praise him highly. Keep this up for several weeks so that it becomes routine and the prescribed area builds up a strong amount of Bobo's scent. He will eventually become used to going only in that area. Your ultimate goal should be to be able to let him out and have him go on his own to the area, eliminate, and come back inside. By limiting where Bobo eliminates to one small area of the yard, you make cleanup much easier and prevent your entire yard from becoming a waste dump that people can't use for recreation. You also are preventing Bobo from thinking that the entire yard is his. It isn't. It is yours, and you have graciously bequeathed one small area to him to use at his discretion.

Solution: Limit Bobo's Freedom in the Home

To underscore the principle that the home is your territory and that Bobo is simply a valued guest there, you should sometimes randomly restrict his freedom to go wherever he wants, whenever he wants. By doing so, you reinforce your status as leader and help reduce his opinion of himself. Selectively restricting Bobo's freedom can also be a way to get him to focus better on you and his environment, and it serves to calm him down. A dog that can go wherever it wants whenever it wants often becomes controlling and self-absorbed. By choosing random times to restrict Bobo's movements, you help keep his attitude in check, thereby limiting dominant displays. It is not punishment, but rather an exercise in authority and self-control.

1. Tether Bobo's lead to a doorknob. Give him a treat, and ignore him for at least half an hour. Give him a chew toy if you want to, but no matter what he does, don't respond. Sit down within sight of him and read a book or watch television. Instruct everyone in the house to ignore Bobo for a half hour.
2. After the half hour, if he is quiet, walk over to him, ask him to sit, and release and praise him. Always make sure you choose a time when he is quiet to release him. If you walk over and pay attention to him while he is barking or throwing a tantrum, you will be rewarding that behavior, so don't do it.
3. Have other members of the family work this exercise, and practice it all over the home. Bobo must learn that he doesn't have to have his nose in everyone's business all the time.

Six

LEADERS PROTECT
THEIR PACKS

The male grizzly lumbered into the meadow at midday, catching the sleepy wolf pack off-guard. At over nine hundred pounds, he came close to weighing more than all the wolves combined. The bear was either not aware of the pack's presence or else didn't care.

The Alpha male caught the scent of grizzly in his sleep and was on his feet before his eyes were fully open. Guided first by his nose, he quickly caught sight of the bear, who was busily digging at some mounded soil about 50 yards to the north, probably looking for grubs or perhaps a marmot in its burrow. Breaking into a full run, the 140-pound timber wolf let out two gruff, percussive sounds that both ended with short, high-pitched howls. It was a vocalization he hadn't used for six summers, and one that his mate, the Alpha female, had never heard before. A sound of dire warning, the call to arms was instantly and instinctively understood by all his brethren to mean that their very existence was in peril.

All looked up from their respective resting places to see their leader sprinting toward a monstrous creature that had been, to most of them, only a myth, a feeling. Now it had come upon them, and their father was running to meet it without hesitation, almost as if the two were old friends. He ran faster than they had ever seen him run, and in a flash the two were together, the bear incredulous at the absurdity of it, this small ghostly dog creature appearing from nowhere and flying toward him like a bee driven to madness by the consumption of its hive. The others were at first frozen by the scene, held back by fear and disbelief. After moments that seemed to her like days, the Alpha female flew to the defense of her husband and was quickly followed by the others, all of them, even the 5-month-old pups. They had all been instantly changed, raised to a level of solidarity that had never been felt before by any of them save the leader and his wife.

The grizzly in his confidence had been slow to react, and he now had two timber wolves hanging from him, one on his back and the other from his right rear leg, their teeth drawing first blood. By the time he could shake them off, he was accosted by five smaller ones, all nipping, growling, and moving fast. The big one on his back had hurt him, he thought. The pain in his bleeding back woke him to his peril. He was angry and needed to hurt these small dog creatures.

The two Alphas kept at a frontal assault while the others bit at the bear's flanks. Not knowing who to attack first, he quickly decided to focus his attention on one wolf at a time. Turning quickly, he lunged at one of the juvenile males, who was caught off-guard. The bear swatted at the young wolf's shoulder, ripping open several long, deep gashes with his 6-inch claws. As he was about to deliver a crushing bite to the small wolf's neck, the Alpha male in an act of desperation lunged at the bear's head, savagely sinking his fangs into his muzzle. The bear rolled to his side, swatted the Alpha female off his right rear leg, and ran uphill to a brace of old cedars. Turning, he rose up to his full height of 10 feet and roared at the growling wolves, who had him flanked on both sides, with both Alphas in front. After a second of indecision, the grizzly dropped back down to all fours and lumbered off into the cedar wood, roaring in disgust and pain.

The wolves came together and licked at each other's wounds. The bleeding had almost stopped. The brave juvenile's wounds would need to be carefully licked clean by the others for the next few days. Both Alphas had lacerations all over their bodies, which each would tend to that night. The young wolves licked at each other and yelped softly. After 20 minutes, most had finally settled. Some were even able to sleep. The Alphas lay next to each other, noses up, rapidly scenting the air, knowing it was not yet time to sleep.

Wolf packs develop a solidarity that rivals or surpasses that of the strongest loyalties found among any group of humans. That instinctive loyalty and devotion is strongest in the leader, who will do anything to protect his pack, including a seemingly suicidal charge on a half-ton grizzly. Any fear he felt was muted by the stronger need to protect his group. As leader, it was his job. So strong is this devotion to duty that he would risk his life if necessary to fulfill his responsibility. Although it may sound melodramatic, it is nonetheless true. Think of how you would react if your children were trapped in a burning building. You would put aside fear and react simply out of parental devotion.

Bobo has these same instincts. He loves you and your "pack" and would defend you all against intruders. Any dog, be it a Maltese or a Malamute, would be ready for trouble if some stranger began pounding away at your door at three in the morning.

As the leader, you must give Bobo the feeling that you are there to protect him, no matter what. You must get him to believe in you and your ability to defend him and to keep him safe from threats, sickness, or injury. If Bobo feels that you are a competent leader, capable of protecting him, he will be less stressed and more confident. A dog that is stressed or worried all the time usually gets that way in part because that is what its owner is like. The dog reflects its leader's mood and tone. If you don't set the standard of leadership for Bobo, he will feel vulnerable and may decide that he has to take charge because no one else will. Many dogs are not capable of this much responsibility, and they become fearful and suspicious of everything and everyone that happens by. Fear aggression can be the result. A fearful dog that thinks it is in charge will bite first and ask questions later. You can avoid the possibility of Bobo showing fear aggression by being a strong, confident leader whom he can look to for guidance and protection.

Goal: To Provide a Safe Environment for Your Dog

As leader of the pack, you must create a safe, secure environment for your dog. A leader must be capable of dealing with unforeseen circumstances and must never put a pack member in needless jeopardy, be it physical or psychological. If you do not take charge, your dog will be forced to, and that might lead to an aggressive incident.

A few years ago, a client called us to relay some sad news about Gerta, her 3-year-old Spaniel mix. It seemed that while her owner was out of the house, Gerta got into a large box of chocolates that had been left out on the coffee table the night before. Chocolate is tempting to dogs because it contains dairy products, sugar, and various oils. Unfortunately, it also contains the chemical *theobromine*, a substance that is extremely toxic to dogs. Gerta scented out the chocolates and proceeded to eat the entire box. Weighing in at only 15 or 20 pounds, the few pounds of chocolate she consumed was enough to prove lethal.

This sad story illustrates how important it is to make the home a safe place for Bobo to live in. Just as you "baby-proof" your home and property to safeguard your child, so must you "dog-proof" your pet's territory to prevent physical or psychological trauma from occurring. Although some dogs never show an interest in potentially dangerous items around the home, most do at some time or other. You must deal with this possibility.

Solution: Safeguard Bobo's Environment

Dogs are curious by nature and are driven to investigate every nook and cranny of their environment. Their excellent sense of smell plays a pivotal role in this function. If an interesting smell wafts out from a kitchen cabinet, rest assured little Bobo will find a way to get in there and check it out. When he does, he will discover many potentially toxic items. The garbage, probably his first target, may contain dangerous items such as chicken bones, broken glass, sharp lids from open cans, or food packaging that Bobo could choke on. At the least, he could end up eating discarded food and getting a bad case of diarrhea.

The garbage, however, is probably the least dangerous item that Bobo could get into under the kitchen sink. Most people also keep a myriad of chemicals here, including ammonia- and bleach-based cleaners, detergents, drain cleaner, furniture polish, house plant fertilizer, and even tarnish removers. All of these products are highly toxic to Bobo, and some, such as the drain cleaner, could be lethal even in minute doses. The simple solution to this problem is to prevent Bobo from ever coming into contact with these items.

First, remove all highly toxic chemicals from beneath the sink and relocate them to a different area, perhaps a high shelf in the garage, a lockable closet, or at least a cupboard located too high for Bobo to reach even if he jumps up on a counter.

Go to the hardware store and purchase child-proof guards for all cupboards, especially the one that houses the garbage. Remember that most dogs have the reasoning capacity of a 2-year-old child, so that any device that can defeat your wandering 2-year-old will probably defeat Bobo. Take care, however, not to use any type of locking device that can be chewed or pawed off by a persistent pooch.

Some owners keep their dogs in the garage or laundry room during the day while they are at work. Both these locations often become storage areas for old paint cans, solvents, detergents, motor oil, antifreeze, wood stain, lawn fertilizer, weed killer, and insecticide: in other words, a veritable gallery of poisons for your dog to pick and choose from. Antifreeze in particular has been responsible for many dog poisonings because its key ingredient, ethylene glycol, has a very sweet taste and attracts dogs like a moth to the flame.

If you must keep Bobo in the garage or the laundry room during the day, make sure all toxic chemicals are either removed or placed up high enough so that he cannot get to them, even by jumping up on counters, cars, or washing machines. If possible, have a lockable storage area for these items, preferably made of metal, as wood can be gradually chewed away by a persistent pet.

The same rules apply to the bathroom. If there are any potentially toxic chemicals such as hair dye, alcohol, iodine, hair relaxers, or "permanent" kits, they should be put into a cupboard equipped with a child-proof lock. In addition, you can keep the bathroom door firmly closed while you are gone.

Electrical appliances can also be a source of great danger to a dog in the home, particularly a young dog that is still in the chewing phase. The electrical cord for your television or VCR can become a lethal weapon if chewed on by Bobo. Make sure access to any cords is made difficult or impossible by hiding them under the carpeting or behind furniture and bookcases. At the same time, provide Bobo with something of his own to chew on, such as a Nylabone or hard rubber toy. Encourage him to chew these, and *firmly* dissuade him from chewing any electrical cords. If necessary, spread a spicy sauce such as Tabasco on a cord that Bobo seems driven to chew on.

Never leave electric irons on, because they can topple off an ironing board and injure Bobo badly. Space heaters and stoves can also cause him injury. When he is alone, either turn these appliances off or confine him to an area away from the potential danger.

When you leave Bobo home alone, make sure you remove any training collars. If a "choke chain" is left on him, he might catch it on a cabinet handle or table leg and end up choking himself. Leaving a regular buckle collar on him is fine provided it is not so loose as to catch on something.

The yard is another area where Bobo may spend a lot of time; therefore, it must be made as safe as your home. Your first consideration should be containment. A securely fenced yard will prevent Bobo from taking off and possibly getting squashed by a car. It will also keep other dogs out of Bobo's territory, preventing any territorial aggression from occurring. Keeping other dogs out of Bobo's yard is your responsibility as leader. You would be remiss if you allowed outsiders to "invade" your pack's territory, which could result in harm to Bobo. At the very least he could become insecure, worrisome, and possibly, dog-aggressive. A fence should be high enough to prevent Bobo from jumping over (or others from jumping in) and low enough to prevent him and others from going under. Take into consideration the breed of dog you have when constructing a fence. An athletic breed such as a Vizsla or Pointer could easily clear a 5-foot fence if it wanted to, so consider a 6-foot fence instead. Terriers, on the other hand, are determined diggers. Their fence needn't be too high, but it should certainly be flush to the ground or even anchored in concrete to prevent the dog from digging under.

Consider a fence that is not transparent to Bobo. Although slightly cheaper than wooden fences, a chain-link fence enables Bobo to see what's going on outside his territory. This may cause him to be concerned: He can see people and animals go by his territory, but he is restricted from doing anything about it because of the fence. A well-constructed wooden fence that Bobo can't see through will remove this worry and create a more secure feeling in Bobo's mind.

Some owners have property that is simply too large to fence in. Many in this position opt for "invisible fencing" to contain their dogs. This system involves burying a series of underground wires around the perimeter of the property and putting a special battery-powered collar on the dog. When Bobo tries to cross the buried wires, he first gets an audible warning. If he ignores this warning and continues, he gets a low-level electrical stimulation that dissuades him from continuing on. Although effective with many dogs, this system tends not to work with dogs that are highly territorial or prey-driven. Rottweilers, for instance, will blow right through invisible fences if they see an intruder or some other challenge to their home. Also, this system does nothing to keep other dogs from coming into your yard and therefore does not serve to protect Bobo in any way. From a leadership standpoint, therefore, this method can be counterproductive.

An option for those who can't afford to fence in a large yard is to build a fenced-in kennel somewhere on the property. A 9- by 12-foot area is more than ample for Bobo. If you choose, you can put down a concrete surface to make cleanup easier. The kennel should be located in a portion of the yard that does not allow Bobo visual access to people coming and going, which could be upsetting to him and perhaps encourage barking. A kennel will also prevent Bobo from digging up your yard in search of bones or burrowing animals. However you structure the yard, it must be a place where constant invasions of the pack's privacy, both physical and visual, are avoided.

Never tie a dog on a chain or rope in the backyard. Dogs that are confined in this fashion can become very stressed. They are able to hear and see things happening, but they can't do anything because of being tied. Many of these dogs run out to the end of the line and bark and growl at some perceived threat, perhaps another dog in the yard next door. When they get to the end of the line, the added tension angers them even more. It is a frustrating feeling for the dog and can promote the development of aggressive behavior. One way that attack dogs are made to be ferocious by their trainers is by using this very method of tying and teasing. You can imagine how frustrating it would be for a dog.

Safeguarding Bobo from poisonous plants is also a concern. Make sure your yard has no toxic plants for him to chew on. Azalea leaves, for example, are toxic to dogs, as are the leaves of the tomato plant. Cedar chip ground cover can also be toxic; a dog that got into the habit of chewing on it could choke. If you are in doubt as to the toxicity of a plant or any type of ground cover material, consult your veterinarian and your local gardening center.

Do not leave any training collars on Bobo while he is in the yard. He could catch the end ring on a rose bush or a tree branch and choke himself.

As leader, you must also ensure that Bobo's extended environment is as safe as possible. For instance, you should not work on any off-leash obedience with him when close to a busy street. He may forget about the presence of speeding cars while chasing his beloved tennis ball and end up getting seriously hurt or killed. Remember, he depends on you to provide him with a safe environment. The same rules go for taking Bobo into an unfamiliar and potentially dangerous environment. If Bobo grew up in the country, it would be unfair of you suddenly to take him onto a busy urban street and expect him to perform a perfect off-leash heel exercise. He might get spooked by a backfire or some other urban distraction and end up running away or getting hit by a bus. Use common sense, and be fair to your dog. Introduce Bobo to new environments gradually, not all at once.

Socialization with other animals is generally a good thing for Bobo, provided it is done in a thoughtful manner. For example, letting your Golden Retriever romp together with a few other friendly dogs in a safe, dog-sanctioned area is fine, whereas leaving your Chihuahua alone with six Rottweilers and three German Shepherds in a small yard would be lethal. Even if nothing bad happened, your actions

would be extremely irresponsible. You would have failed as a leader.
Your poor Chihuahua would probably develop a heart condition as
well.

Before allowing Bobo to interact with other dogs, attempt to find
out if these dogs are friendly. If one of them is an unneutered male,
for instance, chances are he will be fairly territorial and perhaps even
combative. Try to put Bobo with dogs that won't overwhelm him.
For instance, never put a toy dog in with a breed that has a very high
prey drive for small animals, such as a Borzoi or a Siberian Husky.
When possible, get to know the other dogs and their masters. Then,
if everyone gets along, arrange to meet once or twice each week.

As leader, you must also ensure that your dog's safety is not
threatened by wild animals found in and around your neighborhood.
Rats, raccoons, skunks, and squirrels can all carry disease, including
the rabies virus. You should not encourage Bobo to chase or attack
any of these species. All of these animals could be encountered in
parks, on camping trips, or even in your backyard, so be aware.
When in doubt, put Bobo on a leash.

Goal: To Keep Bobo Healthy

As leader, you must not only keep Bobo safe, but also keep him
healthy and fit. He cannot do it on his own. The three general areas
that you should focus on are nutrition, preventative medical care, and
exercise.

Solution: Provide Bobo with a Proper Diet

Ensuring that Bobo receives the proper nutrients is a fairly easy task
these days. Most dry foods available in supermarkets or pet shops
contain all the necessary ingredients to keep Bobo in good shape.
Pet shop foods tend to be of higher quality and cost and contain far
fewer preservatives than do the supermarket brands. They also are
metabolized more completely than supermarket brands, resulting in
smaller stools. You will need to feed Bobo less pet shop food than

supermarket food, because pound for pound, it is more nutritious and caloric.

Food allergies are fairly common among dogs. We have known many dogs, for instance, that were allergic to corn or wheat and some that actually could not tolerate beef. Symptoms of food allergy include skin rashes, diarrhea, vomiting, and hyperactive behavior. Most supermarket brands contain a little of everything, including beef, corn, wheat, chicken, and soy. If Bobo is allergic to any of these, he'll not do well on that food. Switching over to a good pet shop food that focuses on one or two ingredients that Bobo isn't allergic to would be the answer. A lamb and rice diet, for instance, is appropriate for a dog that has an intolerance to corn or beef. If Bobo shows any abnormal reactions to a food, consult your vet immediately. He or she should be able to determine the proper course of action.

Canned foods cost much more per pound than dry foods. Much of their weight is made up of water, which you are paying a premium price for. Many canned foods also contain sugar and preservatives, both of which can adversely affect the behavior of many dogs. If you feel you need to give your dog canned food, do it on a supplementary basis, adding a spoonful or two to Bobo's dry food as a flavor enhancer.

As a general rule, you should follow the manufacturer's recommendations on the food bag with regard to how much to feed. All dogs have different metabolisms, however. Boxers and Pointers are extremely energetic, whereas Bassets and Mastiffs tend to be slow and lazy. A high-energy dog needs to eat more than a lazy dog of the same weight. Also, an older dog needs less food than a young one (although it may want to continue eating the same amount that it did when it was young). As Bobo ages, therefore, you need to reduce the amount given or change over to a food with fewer calories. The metabolism of altered animals is slightly slower than that of nonaltered animals; therefore, they also need to have their amounts cut somewhat. Weighing Bobo every few months is a great idea and will give you insight into his eating habits and level of activity.

Once you find a food that agrees with Bobo, keep him on it. Dogs do not need variety in their diet and can develop diarrhea if their diet is changed too suddenly or frequently. If you have to change Bobo's food, do so gradually, over a period of 2 to 3 weeks.

Avoid giving Bobo pork or chicken bones or any type of bone that splinters. It might puncture his stomach or intestinal tract. Beef knuckle bones do not splinter but can eventually wear down Bobo's canine teeth. Many middle-aged dogs come to our facility with worn teeth as a result of getting too many knuckle bones. It's not fair to Bobo to condemn him to a toothless old age, so if you need to give him bones, do so infrequently, as a special treat.

Solution: Provide Bobo with Proper Preventative Care

As leader, you need to monitor and maintain Bobo's health and take steps to prevent him from acquiring any serious diseases. The first and most important step in this process is developing a good relationship with your veterinarian. A good vet is as valuable as gold. He or she will be able to detect problems with Bobo that may go unnoticed by you and your family. For example, deafness is a common disorder among Dalmatians, and it often goes undetected by owners, who think that their dogs are simply stubborn or aloof. A good vet should catch this problem and direct the owner to a canine behaviorist, who could train dog and owner to deal with the deficiency.

A big part of preventative care is paying attention to Bobo's physical appearance. Many owners don't pay enough attention to notice, for example, that their dog is walking with a limp. We often have an owner come in to board his or her dog with us and discover that it is limping or that its coat looks horrible. The owner sees the dog every day and consequently never takes a good, objective look at the dog. After we point the problem out, however, the owner usually kicks him- or herself for being so blind.

A client brought his 6-year-old Rottweiler, Max, to us because he had begun, seemingly overnight, to growl when petted or touched in any way. Although Rottweilers do have a reputation for not being fond of handling, Max had never been like this before. His temperament had always been closer to that of a Golden Retriever. When the owner came in the door with Max, we quickly noticed that the dog was walking stiffly and seemed to be favoring his left front leg. When we pointed this out to the owner, he thought a minute and then related to us an incident that had occurred a few weeks earlier. Max had been romping in a neighbor's yard with his Labrador Retriever friend, Bo. At one point, Max had jumped off a high rock garden to try to surprise Bo. On landing, he'd let out a cry. The owner walked over to him to see what happened but noticed nothing wrong.

Unfortunately, Rottweilers have the stoic habit of masking pain from injury. Max had hurt himself, but he wasn't showing it. When we examined the dog, it became evident that he had injured his left shoulder in the fall. Any massaging of that area brought a low growl, whereas touching any other area precipitated no response at all. Max had simply begun growling because that was the only way he could think of to stop the pain that came from being touched. We sent him off to the vet, who discovered that Max had a dislocated shoulder. We were amazed that he could have put up with such pain for so long. The owner felt guilty and silly but was grateful for our help. With the aid of his vet, Max healed properly and never showed the growling behavior again.

If you observe your dog with a critical eye at least once each day, you will be able to prevent many health problems from becoming too serious. For example, Bobo might have developed a limp, which could be symptomatic of an injury, arthritis, or hip dysplasia. Or his coat may have lost its sheen, which could point to a worm infestation or food allergy. Excess wax in Bobo's ears could point to an ongoing ear infection; this is something to be aware of as well.

Make sure your vet provides the proper vaccinations for Bobo. Rabies, parvovirus, distemper, leptospirosis, hepatitis, and the corona virus are just some of the diseases that Bobo can be vaccinated against. As leader, it is your responsibility to see to these precautions so that Bobo doesn't have to suffer needlessly. Your vet will set up a proper schedule of vaccinations for Bobo, which should help keep him around for a long time.

Parasites can cause a dog great discomfort. As leader, you must help keep Bobo as free of them as possible. There are many parasites that Bobo could pick up, but the most common ones you will need to deal with are the following:

1. Fleas
2. Ticks
3. Worms

Fleas are nasty little vampirish creatures. They cause Bobo and his dog friends great discomfort, particularly during the summer months. Fleas cause itching, hair loss, rashes, bleeding, and scabbing, and they facilitate the spread of tapeworm. They bother humans as well, getting into your furniture, carpets, and bedding, and biting you in search of blood. Getting rid of them is not an easy task, but as leader you owe it to Bobo to try. Most experts agree that a simultaneous, twofold approach is necessary: Rid the home environment of flea eggs and adult and larval fleas while treating Bobo for his infestation. If you only treat Bobo, the adult fleas in the home will continue to lay eggs. These eggs in the carpeting and bedding will hatch in 7 to 10 days, and they will produce more fleas that will seek out poor Bobo.

Rid your home of fleas by using a commercial flea and tick bomb or by using a flea powder that is sprinkled onto all infested areas of the home, including carpets, dog bedding, and furniture. Also, be sure to vacuum often and change the vacuum cleaner bag frequently. Try keeping a cut-up flea collar inside the bag to deal with the fleas that get sucked into it.

Rid Bobo of fleas by bathing him thoroughly with a good flea shampoo. Obtain one through your vet. Supermarket brands are not as effective. Work the lather deep into Bobo's coat and *allow it to sit on him for at least 5 minutes before rinsing it off.* This is a crucial step that most owners don't do. It is essential to give the lather some time to kill all the fleas instead of just causing them to jump ship. Then, thoroughly rinse Bobo off. Your vet can also provide you with a topical flea spray that can be applied to Bobo after he has been frolicking in a field that you suspect may be infested with fleas. In addition, purchase a fine-toothed flea comb and run it through Bobo's coat once each day during flea season. (Some breeds, such as a Komondor or a Puli, have coats that won't allow a flea comb to pass through, and will need to be bathed more frequently to ensure that their homes are flea-free.) It will turn up fleas, flea eggs, and flea "dirt," which is residue and feces from the fleas. Periodic flea combing will alert you to new infestations that occur, so make a habit of it.

Ticks, although not as common as fleas, can present a serious health problem for Bobo *and* for you. Rocky Mountain spotted fever and Lyme disease are two illnesses that can have serious and lasting effects on humans, often causing long-term and profound lethargy and symptoms of immunodeficiency. Attentiveness to the presence of ticks on Bobo is therefore essential. Ticks are often found in grassy fields and forests during warm weather. They wait for a host to come along and clamp onto it, usually remaining on the victim until satiated, whereupon they drop off. Fortunately, a quick inspection of Bobo will usually reveal their presence. Unlike fleas that scatter quickly, ticks must stay in one location on the host.

If Bobo becomes infested with ticks, the first thing to do is bathe him with a flea and tick shampoo recommended by your vet. This often causes the ticks to drop off or at least loosen their grip. Ticks that remain should be dabbed with alcohol and then carefully removed with tweezers. You must make sure to grasp the tick as close to Bobo's skin as possible. If the head of the tick stays in, the spot may develop a mild infection. Grasp it firmly and pull it out, and then place the tick in a glass of alcohol or burn it. After the evil little vermin have been removed, give Bobo a big cookie for being such a good sport.

Worms can also cause Bobo a great deal of distress. Most live in Bobo's intestinal tract and feed off the nutrients present there. All can cause various distressful symptoms, including lethargy, loss of weight, poor coat, vomiting, and coughing. Observing Bobo's stool on a regular basis can alert you to the presence of most types of worms.

HEARTWORM

Acquired from the bite of a mosquito, the heartworm enters the bloodstream and travels to the heart, where it lives and grows, often to a length of 10 to 12 inches. It will cause Bobo to be lethargic and underweight. He may cough a lot and can ultimately die from the stress put on his heart.

More common in warmer, mosquito-infested climates, heartworm can be avoided by giving the dog pills obtained from your vet. Those living in more temperate climates may not have to worry about heartworm, but it is a good idea to ask your vet about them anyway.

HOOKWORM

Hookworms are intestinal parasites common in puppies, who can get them during nursing. The hookworm can be ingested or acquired through the skin. Dogs infested with this parasite are underweight and sluggish, and they may have a dry, brittle coat. Your vet can detect hookworm infestation through a stool examination and can effectively treat it.

ROUNDWORM

Also located in the gastrointestinal tract, roundworms look like 2-inch-long pieces of vermicelli. They can cause loss of weight, lethargy, diarrhea, and coughing. Common in puppies, this parasite can also be detected in the stool, and it can be effectively treated.

TAPEWORM

Affecting the stomach and intestines, this parasite looks like a grain of rice. It too can cause diarrhea, lethargy, weight loss, and a dry, brittle coat. Easily detected in the stool, tapeworm can be treated fairly simply by your vet.

WHIPWORM

Affecting the large intestine, whipworm can cause diarrhea and exhaustion. Not as apparent to a visual inspection of the stool, whipworm nonetheless can be detected and eliminated.

Solution: Exercise Your Dog

Last year a new client brought his 7-year-old Rottweiler, Naomi, in for boarding. When they came through the door, a hushed silence came over the room. Although she was a small-frame Rottweiler, Naomi weighed almost one hundred and fifty pounds. Truly corpulent, she just about dragged her swollen stomach along the ground. She was so wide, one literally could have draped a tablecloth across her back and served tea on it. We were astonished and alarmed at her condition, and we immediately sat down with the owner to discuss Naomi's extreme obesity, which was so pronounced that her knees and ankles were beginning to buckle under the strain.

Although it was certainly an aberration, Naomi's situation was nevertheless a prime example of poor leadership on the part of the owner. The physical health of your dog is *your* responsibility. Naomi's owner, in addition to drastically overfeeding her, also neglected to exercise her. Naomi spent her days in a small yard and her evenings in the home, never going for walks, swims, or runs, and never playing any games such as fetch. As she became fatter and fatter, exercising her became problematic; she just couldn't do it. We helped her owner implement a 6-month reducing plan involving a substantial reduction in food (particularly treats and leftovers) as well as a gradual increase in activity. Within 5 months, Naomi's weight was down to a much healthier 106 pounds, and she could run and play with the best of them.

Exercise is as crucial to Bobo's health as it is to yours. Dogs that get regular exercise routinely outlive their more sedentary brethren. Even toy dogs such as Papillons and Yorkshire Terriers need to get some form of exercise each day. And just because Bobo spends his entire day in the yard doesn't mean he's doing wind sprints all day.

He's probably spending most of that time sleeping or lying around. Here are some suggestions:

1. Take Bobo for at least two walks each day, even if he's got a big yard to play in. It will be good exercise for both of you, and he'll get to see the real world, something that homebound dogs rarely get to do.

2. Teach your dog to play fetch (see Chapter 3), and play it with him once each day.

3. Take Bobo swimming whenever you can. Swimming is a great exercise that doesn't involve any high-impact stress on the joints. It is a great exercise for dogs with hip dysplasia, arthritis, or any type of structural problem.

4. Take your dog jogging with you. If it's good for you, then it must be good for Bobo. Don't take him, though, if you are planning to run more than a few miles, especially if he is a tiny breed, a big breed, or a breed susceptible to hip dysplasia. Pointers, Huskies, Labs, Goldens, Greyhounds, Poodles, Irish Setters, and Boxers are all breeds that can excel at jogging, whereas Rottweilers, Mastiffs, Saint Bernards, Chihuahuas, Shih Tzus, and Bulldogs may not do as well.

5. Enroll Bobo in a tricks and agility class, where he can learn to run an obstacle course.

6. Take Bobo to a sanctioned dog park and let him run around with several other friendly dogs for an hour or so. He'll have fun exercising and socializing with his own kind, and he will sleep well that night.

7. Take Bobo with you and your family when you go on hiking and camping trips. (Make sure that the area you are going to allows dogs. Most require Bobo to be on a lead all the time.) He will enjoy the fresh air and exercise as much as you and will savor the change of pace.

If you take Bobo into the woods, however, there are some precautions you should take. First, be respectful of other campers and hikers. Do not let Bobo be a pest. Second, always have a lead with you, and use it whenever the law requires or when lots of people are around. A retractable lead will allow Bobo to venture out up to 30 feet from you and yet still be controlled; consider taking one of these along. Do not let Bobo eat plants or animals he happens across, especially mushrooms, which might be toxic. Beware of wild animals as well, particularly snakes. When you get Bobo back home, it might be a good idea to give him a flea and tick bath as well as a visual inspection just to be on the safe side. You might spot a parasite or an injury of some sort that needs attention. Make sure also that you bring enough water and food for Bobo on the trip. He will be running around a lot, and he may need to eat and drink more to compensate.

Seven

LEADERS ARE CALM, FAIR, AND CONFIDENT

The pack rested after eating. The young elk had been taken down by three young males after they discovered it limping across the muddy flood plain of a small alpine lake. By the time the rest of the pack arrived, the three were busily eating.

The Alpha male sauntered over to the kill, sniffing and licking at it while the three young hunters watched, momentarily halting their feeding, not sure if they should surrender their hard-earned privilege. Then, the Alpha male walked off a few paces and lay down, content to watch the three fledgling hunters enjoy their first kill together.

The rest of the pack tentatively joined the three young males, who by now had each eaten close to their fill. The Alpha male came over to join in on the meal. He was impressed at the size of the juveniles' first kill and at their initiative. To show his respect, he had allowed these three first-feeding privileges. Confident in his leadership, he knew that they would not interpret his acquiescence as weakness, but rather as tribute to their success. It was the fair thing to do.

The leader of a wolf pack is not a tyrant, but rather a benevolent dictator and an efficient administrator. He should not steal from a subordinate, discipline irrationally, lose his temper, or show any signs of fear toward pack members or outsiders. Proper leadership instills confidence into the pack, rewards initiative, and operates in a consistent, predictable manner. If the Alpha male were skittish, temperamental, and unfair, pack unity would quickly deteriorate, resulting in a diminished level of teamwork. Ultimately, a high mortality rate among the young would follow, threatening the very survival of the species. Responsible leadership involves not only authority, therefore, but also knowing how to raise the confidence level of subordinates by acting in a fair and reasonable manner.

The Alpha male wants the other members of the pack to obey him, but he also wants them to become capable and sure of their own abilities. He allowed them to feed first. The young hunters all knew that their leader was very capable and could have fed first had he wanted to. His refusal to do so was interpreted by them not as weakness but as tribute and praise. Because he was a strong leader and in no way threatened, he could be sure that the young wolves would not interpret his acquiescence as weakness.

As leader of your pack, you must set a good example for Bobo. Avoiding temper tantrums and irrational emotion, exuding confidence, and treating those around you fairly will help solidify you as a true leader and not just a big bully. Intimidation is *not* leadership, but simply physical domination that lowers confidence and fosters a climate of fear. A dog that is lorded over by a hard, unfair, emotional person will obey out of fear, but it will be scared of strangers, other dogs, and new situations. It will also have no genuine respect for its owner and very little loyalty. Dogs that are mistreated in this way by bullying owners often run away or develop profound fear-aggressive tendencies, much in the same way that abused children so often end up as violent offenders.

Goal: Provide an Atmosphere of Fairness

The leader of the pack should be calm, fair, and confident in all interactions with his or her dog. This chapter illustrates easy ways for owners to create an atmosphere of confidence, respect, and fairness between them and their dog. After creating this mind-set, the owner will find Bobo to be more predictable, respectful, pleasant to be with, and able to deal with the unexpected.

Joe, a client of ours, always felt that dogs should be controlled with a firm hand. When he adopted Roxy, therefore, a Lab/Shepherd–cross puppy, he immediately began laying down the law. Whenever Roxy had an accident in the house (an almost everyday occurrence), Joe would shove her face in it, spank her bottom, and toss her outside into the yard. He fed her in the yard and had her sleep out there too, feeling that was where dogs belonged. When Roxy was about 12 weeks old, Joe went out and purchased a pronged training collar for her and began walking her around the neighborhood with it, yanking away at her lead if she pulled or tried to jump on strangers.

By the time Roxy was 7 months old, she had developed lick sores on her front feet. It turned out that when she was alone in the yard, she would incessantly lick and nip at her paws until they became raw and infected. Thinking that Roxy had a skin condition, Joe took her to the vet to have it checked out. The vet quickly diagnosed the problem and informed Joe that the cause was stress. She then recommended that he come to us for an evaluation.

After speaking to Joe and getting a feel for the situation, we realized that Roxy was being unfairly treated. Joe was not purposefully being cruel to her. He just had an antiquated idea of how to treat dogs, possibly learned from a parent or grandparent while he was a child living on a farm in eastern Washington state. With as much tact as possible, we pointed out his mistakes and how they had led to Roxy's condition. First, his martial attitude toward Roxy was completely uncalled for. She was a submissive, mild-tempered dog who wouldn't hurt a fly. Joe's techniques, appropriate for lion taming, were disastrous when applied to poor Roxy. The "shove her face in it" house-training technique, an "old school" method, certainly didn't work with Roxy, serving only to terrorize her and make her afraid of eliminating.

The use of a pronged training collar, normally needed only with very strong, pushy dogs, was extreme overkill in Roxy's case and further served to create a mind-set of fear and dread in her. Isolating her in the yard most of the day also contributed to her paranoia. Dogs are social creatures that need interaction with others in order to be content. Denied access to the "pack" and to its "den," Roxy slipped further and further into an emotional funk.

We pointed out all these factors to Joe and made him realize that the lick sores were Roxy's way of releasing the stress that Joe's martial techniques had precipitated. We told him to lighten up, to get Roxy into the house more, and to work on some positive reinforcement techniques, especially praising and offering treats as rewards for appropriate behavior. We advised him not to use the pronged collar and to cease shoving her face into her stool. We pointed out that Roxy was still having accidents in the house, so the technique must not be working all that well. Joe ingested all this information and, feeling a bit guilty, promised to change his ways.

A month later he came back to us, saying that he had tried to change, but that he'd not had much luck. Roxy's lick sores were even worse. We advised that he consider finding a more appropriate home for Roxy. After a few days of introspection, he agreed. We put him in touch with a retired couple looking for a quiet, sweet dog. Roxy took an immediate liking to them, and the match worked out perfectly. We also helped Joe find his perfect dog: A family had recently put their 2-year-old Bullmastiff, Mac, up for adoption because of his extremely dominant nature. Joe's personality was better suited to a dog like Mac, so we got them together and it worked out well.

Joe had been unfair to Roxy and a *poor leader*. Rather than instilling confidence into her, he caused her to be stressed and to worry. Roxy was isolated, lonely, and fearful all the time. Joe was unfair to her, a trait unbecoming to a leader. It was a classic mismatch of dog to owner. Joe's ability to admit his shortcomings was admirable, and he was quickly rewarded through the adoption of Mac, a dog custom-tailored to Joe's personality. Mac needed a firm, stoic leader. By requiring him to take Mac through a basic obedience class as a condition of the adoption, we showed Joe how to create a fair, close bond with Mac. Roxy was much more at ease with the retired couple; her lick sores healed and never came back.

————

Bobo is an emotional creature. He shows happiness, anger, fear, expectation, and concern, just as humans do. Our shared emotionality is one of the reasons humans and canines enjoy each other so much. Both humans and canines are pack-oriented animals. The need to be with others is innately understood by both. Bobo doesn't hold onto, or dwell on, thoughts for a long time, however, the way we can. He also doesn't think in abstract terms, but instead thinks concretely, or in the moment. He is not capable of understanding how his actions can affect others. Emotional events, be they happy, sad, or annoying, won't stay with him for very long. He also won't take things as personally as we might, and he certainly won't hold a grudge. A few minutes after a dominance confrontation with another dog, Bobo completely lets go of it, and both dogs can continue to interact without much fear of reprisal. Dogs are very fair amongst themselves. A quick confrontation settles an issue of dominance, and both dogs abide by the rules without pride becoming a factor.

Not so with humans. We are not quite as predictable, and we certainly tend to dwell more on emotional events than do our canine companions. We brood and rationalize and often unfairly target others as the source of our unhappiness. In our interactions with dogs, we tend to allow our human emotionality to control how we relate instead of adopting Bobo's more facile, predictable style. He doesn't understand grudges, irrational emotional outbursts, or undue verbal or physical abuse. Bobo is instinctively more fair-minded than humans.

Owners who use overly emotional techniques on their dogs confuse them and create in them a profound sense of insecurity, which often leads to numerous behavioral problems, including fear aggression. Most often, an owner will lose his or her temper long after a dog has done something wrong. The prime example of this is when an owner comes home to find a valued item such as an expensive shoe chewed to bits. The overwhelmingly common reaction is to seek out Bobo and yell at him or, in extreme cases, hit the dog (of which we entirely disapprove). Humans assume that Bobo realized the destruction of the shoe was wrong and that he sat around for hours thinking about it. That is a truly presumptuous, "species-ist" way of thinking. The truth is that Bobo did the deed and then more or less forgot about it 10 minutes later. Remember, dogs live in the moment, don't think in the abstract, and easily forget an event that occurred just a few moments before.

Bobo's owner finds the destroyed shoe, calls him over, and screams bloody murder at him, thinking that Bobo can equate this emotional tirade with the mangling of the shoe. In reality, all Bobo understands is that you came home and yelled at him. Therefore, in Bobo's mind, the act of you *coming home* becomes a dreaded event. Bobo has no clue that something he did *6 hours ago* is the cause of your displeasure. In his mind, he is thinking, "Oh, no, here he comes . . . he's putting the key in the door . . . last time he came home he walked in and just started screaming his head off at me, so why should today be any different? I'd better hide somewhere before he sees me." You must not assume that your reason for being upset is clear to Bobo. Remember, he is not human. His building anxiety could easily end up being displaced during the day in the form of *more* destructive chewing episodes while he is alone, waiting for that tense moment when you walk through the door and scream your head off.

Solution: Avoid Extremes of Emotion

The Alpha leader rarely loses his temper with other members of the pack. Extreme emotion tends to create disharmony and great stress, resulting in a loss of teamwork and trust. Even when the Alpha leader finds it necessary to come down hard on another member of the pack, the event is over quickly, and both parties soon forgive and forget.

Losing your temper only serves to upset and confuse Bobo and to lower your status as leader. A leader is trusted by the pack. If Bobo can't predict whether you will be happy, sad, or angry with him, he will ultimately lose faith in you and become insecure. Intimidation, yelling, and physical force may succeed in temporarily controlling Bobo, but they will ultimately destroy the bond of trust between you. Bobo will dread your presence instead of longing for it.

Try also to avoid the other end of the emotional spectrum. Do not fawn all over or baby Bobo or go into a frenetic, overly happy state. Such behavior serves only to overly excite Bobo and shut down his brain. By placating and spoiling Bobo, you will in effect reduce his ability to deal with the outside world. A child who is pampered its whole life, when suddenly thrust into the real world will not be able to cope efficiently with responsibilities and challenges that await. The same goes for Bobo. Don't spoil him if you want him to be confident and well-adjusted. Maintaining a loving yet even temper with Bobo will keep him thinking and build his trust in you.

Solution: Don't Set Bobo up to Fail

If you have to leave Bobo alone for a while and you know he has a history of destructive behavior, don't leave him in an area where he can do any type of damage. If he likes to chew shoes (a favorite because they are made of leather and are inundated with your scent), pick them up and store them away where they belong. The same goes for anything else Bobo is likely to chew, including remote controls, belts, clothing, eyeglasses, hairbrushes, and so on. Remove all of these from Bobo's area, and provide him with a few chew toys of his own to amuse himself with. Leave Bobo in an area where he simply cannot do damage.

The same principle applies if Bobo has a house-training problem. If you know he is not reliably house-trained, why set him up to fail by leaving him alone with access to the entire home? He *will* have an accident, and you *will* lose your temper when you come home 6 hours later. Of course, Bobo won't connect your anger with the accident because it occurred, in dog terms, ages ago. Instead, *prevent* him from having an accident in the home by either keeping him outside, containing him in a travel crate, or confining him to a small area of the home while you are out (see the section on crate training in Chapter 5). If you don't set Bobo up to fail, you'll have no reason to blow your cool, thereby avoiding an unproductive emotional scene.

If you know that Bobo tends to bark at strangers when left outside, don't leave him in an area where he can see people walking by all day. You will just be making the barking problem worse and setting Bobo up for a good "talking to" after you learn of his barking from your neighbor, perhaps 3 days after the fact. Think about it from Bobo's point of view: He is in the yard, and he can see the sidewalk through the chain-link fence. He sees someone walking toward the house and he barks, out of his instinctive desire to protect his territory. So what happens? The person continues to walk on, eventually passing the house and disappearing down the street. In Bobo's mind, *he thinks that his barking chased the intruder away.* He has convinced himself that barking *works,* and he will do it again, only louder next time. He doesn't realize that the "invader" would have disappeared even if he'd kept his big barker shut tight. The solution is simply to put him in the house during the day, restrict him to a section of the yard that does not allow visual access to people going by, or get a fence that he cannot see through.

If you know that Bobo does not like being petted by strangers, don't force him to endure this. We had a client a few years ago who owned a beautiful 3-year-old Saluki named Tasha, who had always been skittish around lots of strange people. Sight hounds in general tend to be more aloof than other breeds and do not savor the idea of people coming up and touching them. Tasha was even more sensitive to this than was normal for her breed. Her owner simply could not accept Tasha's antisocial leanings. She was a very outgoing individual and probably should have chosen a Golden Retriever instead of a Saluki. She would constantly take Tasha for walks on busy city streets and encourage passersby to pet her. It became too much for the dog, who began snapping and growling at people who came near.

When the owner brought Tasha in to see us for an evaluation, we explained to her the breed's tendency to be aloof and that asking Tasha to act like a Golden Retriever was simply unfair. The owner was, in fact, setting Tasha up to fail. She had overly high expectations that the dog could not fulfill, largely because of breed-specific behavior. We instructed her to arrange less confrontational forms of socialization for Tasha that wouldn't overload her and cause panic. We suggested that she have a few neighbors come over for coffee twice each week. Each person could come in, drop a cookie on the floor, and then ignore Tasha unless she came over to them for attention. Having a neighbor walk Tasha once each week in a quiet area also helped get her used to being with other people. The idea is not to place your dog into any situation in which it has no chance of succeeding.

Solution: Don't Hold Grudges

When the Alpha male in a wolf pack has to discipline a pack member, he does it quickly and then is done with it. He doesn't brood on the situation. He deals with it and forgets it. As leader, you need to take the same attitude. If Bobo does something bad and *you catch him doing it*, deal with the situation and *let it go*. If he eats a forty-dollar belt, there is no sense in holding a grudge for days. He won't understand and will instead become insecure and unsure of your leadership. Deal with a problem with as little anger and emotion as possible, and then move on.

Solution: Know What to Expect

The owner of a 2-year-old German Shepherd female named Flora came to us once for help in alleviating his dog's insecurity around other dogs. She was a nervous dog and seemed always to expect a bad experience to be right around the corner. Flora was a nice dog, though, provided nothing unpredictable occurred. We felt sorry for her; she wanted to relax but couldn't.

After quizzing the owner on Flora's background history and daily routine, we learned that part of their daily walk brought them into a neighborhood that had numerous dogs loose in their front yards. Whenever anyone would walk by, these dogs would charge their fences and bark bloody murder. Flora's owner found these territorial displays to be quite unnerving and got into the habit of crossing streets and jogging quickly by when confronted with this situation. He'd admitted to being scared on more than one occasion. We concluded that Flora, already a sensitive dog by nature, had picked up on her master's lack of confidence during these walks and, lacking a confident leader to look up to and protect her, had become even more nervous and unsure. We explained to the owner what was occurring and how his own fear was amplifying Flora's problem. We recommended that he avoid the questionable neighborhood and begin socializing Flora in a tricks and agility class, which is normally filled with happy dogs and owners learning to have fun together. Within a few months, Flora was able to relax and have fun with the other dogs.

Don't place yourself and Bobo into situations that may be potentially dangerous or that you know you can't handle. If you are walking him, choose a route that is in a relatively safe area, one that is well-lighted and familiar to you. Don't choose a route that tends to have lots of stray or off-leash dogs roaming about. Avoid unsavory crowds of people or anything else you think you might have trouble dealing with.

If you do confront an unknown such as a stray dog or a stranger, remain calm and *deal with it.* If you show fear, Bobo will sense it immediately and become insecure or perhaps even fear-aggressive. On the other hand, if Bobo sees you confidently deal with the outsider, the experience will instill confidence in him. If a stray or off-leash dog shows interest in you and Bobo, continue walking while observing its intentions. A stray normally is very cautious and probably won't approach closely, whereas an off-leash dog may live nearby and will be more daring because of his instinctive desire to protect his territory. Either way, continue walking, avoid eye contact, and talk to the strange dog in an upbeat, positive tone. If the dog shows any aggressive intent, try telling it in a commanding voice "no!" or "go home!"

In rare circumstances, you may have to defend yourself with a stick or rock. Ninety-nine percent of the time, however, this won't be necessary. If the dog *does* attack Bobo, *do not break up* the fight *yourself;* you may be bitten. If your neighborhood has lots of loose dogs roaming around, it might be wise to carry a walking stick or some pepper spray, just in case. The whole idea is to *deal with the situation,* the way any leader would.

When you encounter people while with Bobo, *you* should greet them, not him. Let Bobo see that this is someone you approve of, to put him at ease. If it isn't someone you know or care to greet, just walk by confidently with Bobo. Don't slow down or show fear. Continue on as if there is nothing to worry about. If the person seems a bit unsavory, give him or her a wide berth and continue on. The idea is to let Bobo feel that *you have a handle on the situation.* If you show fear or weakness, you will lose status points and cause Bobo to feel insecure, which could lead to his worrying when passersby, joggers, or other dogs come close to him. Of course, your own confidence level should be boosted by the fact that you have your trusty companion Bobo with you. Rest assured that if someone or something really did attack you, the chances are he'd come to your aid.

Solution: Decide and Act

The Alpha wolf decides on a course of action and then acts on it. There is rarely indecision or uncertainty. He makes a decision and then carries it out. The pack is comforted by this. They know they can count on him to act with purpose, in any circumstance.

As leader of your pack, you must reflect this attitude. Be decisive. Choose a course of action and see it through. If you ask Bobo to sit, *keep at it* until he sits. If he is on the sofa and shouldn't be, don't wait 10 minutes to get him off it. Just do it. He'll respect you for it. Doubt and indecision are not qualities that Bobo will admire in you. Decide and act. Good leaders always do.

Solution: Be Consistent

Dogs prefer some routine in their lives. They like to do things at the same time and in the same fashion. Irregularity can be confusing to them. If a leader shows inconsistent behavior, the pack is apt to see this as a weakness, creating confusion and disharmony.

Be consistent with Bobo. If one of your rules is *no dogs on the bed*, stick to it. Don't sometimes let Bobo up on the bed but other times yell at him for doing it. If you let him jump up on you when you come home from work but yell at him for jumping on a guest, you are being unfair and inconsistent. A dominant, pushy dog needs rules. Set them up and stick to them. Try to maintain a sense of regularity in Bobo's life.

Solution: Manage Relationships Between Dogs in Your Household

Many homes have more than one dog. The rules of leadership must still apply. You are the leader to all of them, just as the Alpha wolf is to his pack, which often contains over a dozen members.

Being fair, however, doesn't mean being democratic. Owners of multiple dogs often make a common error with regard to the way they control their "pack." Many attempt to foster a democratic dynamic among the members, forgetting that dogs instinctively try to form their own dominance hierarchy. Owners often want to give equal rights and status to all their dogs, ignoring the fact that the more dominant animal should be afforded more respect and privilege *because* of its dominant position.

For example, let's say that we have two dogs, Bobo and Sid, living in the same home, with Bobo clearly the dominant one. One day Bobo and Sid come into the house to find that their owner has placed a nice new dog toy on the floor for them to play with. Sid, the subordinate one, gets to it first, but Bobo immediately walks over, grumbles at Sid, and takes the toy. Their owner sees what happened, decides that Bobo was being a big bully, and proceeds to punish him and let Sid have the toy. Guess who was dead wrong here. Yes, the owner. As the dominant dog, Bobo had the right to investigate the toy first. Sid chose to ignore that and was quickly taught a lesson by Bobo.

There was no injustice about it. The two dogs were working it out between themselves until the owner interfered. Had Bobo investigated then lost interest in the toy, there would have been no problem with Sid claiming it as his own. The owner should have ignored the incident, but instead punished Bobo, the dominant dog, for doing what he had the right to do according to canine law. The owner created confusion and disharmony among the pack.

The owner of multiple dogs should allow them to work out their own pecking order and then *support* that order. The dominant dog will want to be petted first, will want to eat first, and will want the right to investigate new situations first. As the owner, you should support this. Put the dominant dog's food bowl down first. Allow it to sleep higher than the other dogs if it so chooses. Clip its leash on first when preparing to take the dogs for a walk. Pet it first. Give it the first treat. You won't be playing favorites. You'll just be reinforcing the pack dynamic, which is not democratic but hierarchical.

The exception to the basic rule of letting dogs work out their own pecking order would be if *severe* aggression is occurring on a regular basis between them. If, for instance, you have had one fairly dominant dog for years and then adopt another adult dog of equal or greater dominance, the possibility of serious aggression between them may be high enough to require you to take a more active role in monitoring their interactions. Regular obedience training sessions involving both dogs would be necessary to keep the peace while they gradually worked out the dynamics of their relationship. If the relationship between your dogs goes from simple posturing and grumbling at each other to true, bloody aggression, you must put a stop to it by isolating them from each other. Then, call a professional canine behaviorist for help.

Ideally, you must allow your dogs to work out their own pecking order. To do anything else would be unfair treatment, and poor leadership.

Eight

WHAT NEXT?

Chances are, if you have consistently followed the advice in Chapters 1 through 7 for at least 6 to 8 weeks, you have noticed dramatic changes occur in your relationship with Bobo. He now sees you not only as friend and benefactor, but as his leader as well. When a dog truly recognizes someone as its leader, it will *want* to obey and please that person. That's why dogs are relatively easy to train in comparison to cats. Cats, although intelligent, have no real pack loyalties and live a profoundly independent, self-centered life. They are charming narcissists, if you will. A dog, on the other hand, on identifying its pack hierarchy and leader, will strive to fit in and help keep things stable.

Bobo is now respecting your leadership and behaving one hundred percent better. Now what? We have some suggestions that will not only help maintain the new relationship but improve it as well.

Continuance of All Leadership Principles

The exercises and suggestions in Chapters 1 through 7 were not meant to be quick fixes. They are instead lifestyle changes that should be adhered to for the life of your dog, if you want to maintain the proper relationship between you. The basic tenets should be maintained:

1. Eat before Bobo.
2. Sleep higher than Bobo.

3. Initiate and control interactions.
4. Go first, not last.
5. Control all space in the home.
6. Maintain a dominant posture.
7. Begin and end play.
8. Be fair, calm, and confident.
9. Be a good provider and protector.

After the initial 6- to 8-week period, you can begin to ease up slightly on some aspects of the training. For instance, you can probably reduce the frequency of tethering and crating and see what effect this has on Bobo's behavior. If Bobo remains respectful and doesn't resume jumping up on you or the beds and furniture, stealing your possessions, or having house-training problems, the restriction of his access to specific areas can be relaxed. Also, instead of *never* allowing him access to your lap, bed, or sofa, you might try (if you desire) teaching him to come up *on command only*. The use in the home of the 8- to 10-foot lead can also be reduced over time, if Bobo is doing well. Use your best judgment. If Bobo slips up, go back to consistent work in that area. Some extremely dominant, pushy dogs, however, are too set in their ways to be cut any slack.

Obedience Training

As we stated earlier in the book, taking a basic obedience class with Bobo will vastly improve your chances of establishing leadership and reforming his dominant nature. Performing our leadership exercises will help change Bobo's opinion of you, readjust his opinion of himself, and generally create a more natural dynamic between you. Obedience training will give you additional tools with which to control Bobo, thereby helping to increase your leadership status even more. Think of leadership in terms of *proper tone and attitude* and of obedience as *mechanics and content*. Each complements the other. Excellent obedience will not be possible, however, without the existence of excellent leadership.

In a basic obedience class, Bobo should learn to sit, lie down, come, stay, "leave it," walk on a loose lead, and heel. Some classes also discuss canine behavior, nutrition, games, and leadership. One of the big advantages to taking a class is the socialization that occurs. Bobo will get to meet with ten to fifteen other dogs and people on a weekly basis. Most dogs never get to experience this level of socialization. It is an essential ingredient in building Bobo's confidence, and it could be the most positive experience of his life. You will get to see ten to fifteen other owners relating to their dogs, and you will learn more about dog/owner dynamics than you ever have before. You also might end up making some friends for yourself *and* Bobo. By all means, take Bobo to school, and don't wait until he's 8 years old to do it.

If you choose a class and, after attending one or two sessions, do not feel comfortable with the methods used or the atmosphere, trust your instincts and find another class. Most instructors know their stuff, but there are some bad ones out there, so be selective.

After Bobo graduates from a basic obedience class, consider continuing on to an advanced class, where Bobo will begin to learn how to perform his obedience more efficiently, with less input from you. Off-lead behavior will be perfected, as will performing under increasing levels of distraction. The instructor also may begin encouraging you to come up with your own ideas and methods. By this stage, you and Bobo will begin learning how to work together as a team. He will do things for you because he wants to and not because he has to. All the while, your position as leader will be solidified even more. By the time the two of you make it through an advanced obedience class, any problem you once had with Bobo should be just a bad memory.

Consider also taking classes that teach tricks and agility work. As mentioned in Chapter 3, Bobo will love learning tricks because only positive motivations are used. You get Bobo to learn because it's fun, not because he has to conform. It is also an opportunity for you to learn to create your own methods and set your own agenda. The number of tricks taught is limited only by your imagination. Agility classes will improve Bobo's coordination and aerobic health. He will have a ball as well, darting in, out, or over tunnels, ramps, weave poles, seesaws, and high jumps.

Once Bobo's obedience training is solid, consider entering him in an obedience competition. Usually sponsored by the American Kennel Club (AKC) or the United Kennel Club (UKC), these shows are organized in a three-tiered fashion. The *novice level* is easiest, followed by the more intermediate *open level* and the advanced *utility level*. Those that pass the test in the novice class are awarded a "Companion Dog" certificate, or CD (in the United Kennel Club, this certificate is called a UCD). To achieve this certificate, Bobo will have to perform perfectly all basic obedience techniques, on- and off-lead, with lots of distractions going on. It isn't an easy title to win.

The next level, the open category, is much more difficult, requiring the dog to perform:

1. off-lead healing
2. retrieving over flat ground and a high jump
3. a broad jump
4. a quick "drop" or down, halfway through a recall
5. rock-solid stays while you are out of the room

Dogs that succeed are rewarded with the "Companion Dog, Excellent" certificate, or CDX (the United Kennel Club calls theirs a UCDX). The highest level of competition is the utility class, which tests scent discrimination, directed retrieve and jumping, signal command comprehension, and much more. Some dogs take years to achieve this level; most never succeed. Those that do are awarded the "Utility Dog" certificate, or UD (UUD in the United Kennel Club).

If Bobo is purebred, you might also consider having him compete in breed "conformation" shows. Winning dogs have the best appearance and structures among those in their respective breeds or groups. Although this competition is not dependent on obedience, Bobo will have to be compliant and well-socialized to do well in these contests. They must be unaltered to show in conformation shows.

There are numerous mixed-breed obedience shows as well. Mixed-breed obedience clubs have sprung up all over the country and celebrate the intelligence and physical abilities of our mongrel companions. The United Kennel Club also sponsors obedience competitions for mixed-breed dogs.

Variation in Routine

Once Bobo is completely accepting of your leadership and behaving well, you should begin to think about varying his routine somewhat. By introducing new methods and new experiences into his life, you will be able to verify whether Bobo is truly respectful of and confident in your leadership. For example, after 6 to 8 weeks of following the leadership exercises in this book, try the following experiment. Instead of taking Bobo for a walk each day at 6:30 P.M., delay it until 7 or 8 and see what happens.

Try taking him for a walk in a different neighborhood and see what his reaction is. Does he flip out or remain calm and curious? Try randomly asking him to do things you wouldn't normally require of him, such as staying in the middle of the living room for 20 minutes while you go about your business. Or introduce unusual, new distractions and see what effects they have on Bobo. Does the sound of escaping air from a balloon cause him to panic, or does he take it in stride? Does a friend walking by with a box on her head cause him to go crazy, or does he look at her and you as if you were both nuts? Try letting a friend Bobo doesn't know very well walk him down the street. What is his reaction? Coming up with odd variations of the status quo can check, or "proof," your leadership over Bobo as well as measure his depth of confidence and adaptability.

Socialization

Bobo should be allowed to interact with as many people and other dogs as possible, from as early an age as possible. Unfortunately, many owners don't allow this to happen, for several reasons. Some don't dare take their dogs out in public because their manners are atrocious or they are too aggressive or fearful. Others simply fall into a rut with their dogs and don't seem to have the time or inclination to get the dogs out and away from the home. Most of us come home from work, eat dinner, feed the dog, and spend what little time remains in the day with family. We retire and then get up the next morning to start the whole process over again. When the weekend comes around, we are anxious to go out and have some fun. We get together with friends, go to a movie or for a hike, or take a trip to the beach. While frantically trying to have some fun before work begins again Monday morning, we leave our dogs home, the same place they've been all week. They don't get to meet new dogs or people and instead slowly develop a siege mentality. A hermit who isolates himself from the world eventually becomes suspicious of others and extremely distrustful. The same can happen to Bobo if you force him to live a cloistered existence at home.

From the time he is very young, you should get Bobo out into the world and away from home as much as possible. Do not allow Bobo to interact too heavily with the outside world until he is past 11 weeks of age, however, the time when the "fear imprint" stage is over. Anything frightening or disturbing that happens to the dog during that stage, which lasts from the eighth to the eleventh week, may have a lasting and deleterious effect on him. After this period, however, you should take him for walks down active residential streets, let him see people and cars, and allow him to hear the sounds of his world. Do not do this to the point of stressing your puppy. If he shows signs of stress, back off and socialize him more slowly. Give your mail carrier a box of dog biscuits and ask him or her to drop one at Bobo's feet each day. Do the same with guests coming into your home. Let Bobo interact with other dogs or even a cat or two. In most circumstances, this opening up of Bobo's environment will increase his confidence and make him happier.

There are exceptions. If Bobo is already extremely antisocial or fearful of strangers, don't force him to go out among them to get petted. This would be unfair and cruel on your part. Shy or timid dogs *can* be taken out to parks and regularly walked within sight of activity without having close contact. This is a good way of easing them into the real world. Dogs like this should never be forced to interact.

Likewise, if Bobo is very dog-aggressive, don't force him to interact closely with other dogs. Take him instead to an area where there are dogs on-lead and let Bobo see them from a distance. Gradually he will learn to accept their presence, provided they don't come into his space.

Getting a Second Dog

The acquisition of a second dog may have a beneficial effect on Bobo. If he spends lots of time alone, the addition of an appropriate friend might brighten up his days. If Bobo has gone through all the leadership exercises and gets along well with other dogs, he could become a good role model for a new puppy, who will learn how to comport himself properly from "big brother Bobo." Having a well-behaved, confident, respectful dog can be the best way to acclimate a new dog to the home. If you decide to adopt an older dog, there will be a period of adjustment of several weeks for both animals. Expect some posturing and arguments, but try to let them work it out themselves. Eventually they should both be happy for the company. Just make sure that Bobo is well-behaved before you add another member to the pack.

The Aging Dog

As the leader of your pack, you must take into consideration the changes that Bobo will go through as he begins to age. Once he reaches 7 or 8 years, he will begin to slow down somewhat. You must consider reducing the amount of strenuous exercise he gets, especially if he is beginning to get stiff in the hips or shoulders. If you have been jogging 5 miles with him every day, consider taking shorter runs each day. If he likes to go hiking with you, try not to let him leap off high places, even if he is used to doing so. There will come a time when he'll *think* he can still do it but might hurt himself in the process.

Bobo's metabolism will begin to slow down somewhat. You will need to decrease his food allotment slightly or give him a food with fewer calories to prevent obesity. Excess weight on a dog can easily exacerbate any structural problems that it might be suffering from. Remember, seeing to Bobo's health and well-being is a big part of your job as leader.

Bobo may experience other health problems as he ages. Watch for the development of allergies to food, plants, or other substances in his environment. Changes in coat or skin condition can be indicative of this. Keep an eye on his eating habits as he ages. Old dogs that suddenly start eating less or not at all might be developing some form of cancer or other internal problem. Be aware of changes in Bobo's elimination patterns as well. Older dogs often develop urinary tract infections, ulcers, diabetes, thyroid conditions, intestinal blockages, or fatty tumors.

You may need to supply Bobo with a soft bed or blanket as he ages to ease the discomfort of arthritis and to insulate him better from a cold floor. If he seems to get cold more easily, don't hesitate to get him a doggie sweater. Make sure to continue taking him to the vet on a regular basis. He or she will be able to help you keep old Bobo around as long as possible.

A Final Word

We hope this book has aided you in getting Bobo to become a more enjoyable, obedient pet. A dog that is well-behaved and respectful can be a wonderful, comforting presence to you and your family. By following the suggestions contained within, you can begin to understand just what a joy dogs can be and how rewarding it can be to lead them.

The Alpha male woke up suddenly and looked around at his sleeping pack. The morning was still hours away, and all the others were fast asleep. He arose and walked quietly over to the two pups sleeping in a tangle near their mother, sniffed them both, then lay down. The moon was nearly full; he looked up at it and yawned. A warm breeze began to blow through the cedars as he began to drift back into a peaceful sleep.

Nancy Baer, a lifelong resident of the Northwest, is currently the owner/operator of A *Canine Experience*, a learning institution dedicated to the training of people who want to become professional dog trainers. Nancy has trained thousands of dogs and people in her career, and has participated in most aspects of dog training, including solving behavioral problems, obedience competition, hunting, and scent work. She lives in Snohomish, Washington.

Steve Duno, a native New Yorker, is a freelance writer and canine behaviorist. He currently resides in Seattle, Washington.